Oxford School Shakespeare

A Midsummer Night's Dream

edited by

Roma Gill, OBE
M.A. *Cantab.*, B. Litt. *Oxon.*

Oxford University Press

Oxford University Press, Great Clarendon Street, Oxford OX2 6DP

Oxford   New York   Athens   Auckland   Bangkok   Bogota
Bombay   Buenos Aires   Calcutta   Cape Town   Dar es Salaam
Delhi   Florence   Hong Kong   Istanbul   Karachi   Kuala Lumpur
Madras   Madrid   Melbourne   Mexico City   Nairobi   Paris
Singapore   Taipei   Tokyo   Toronto   Warsaw
and associated companies in
Berlin   Ibadan

Oxford is a trade mark of Oxford University Press

© Oxford University Press 1981
Reprinted 1984, 1985, 1986, 1987, 1990, 1991
This revised edition first published 1992
Reprinted 1992, 1993, 1994, 1995, 1996, 1997 (twice), 1998, 1999
Trade edition first published 1994
Reprinted 1997, 1998 twice

ISBN 0 19 831975 4 (school edition)
ISBN 0 19 831982 7 (trade edition)

Illustrations by Shirley Tourret

Cover photograph by Laurence Burns shows Judith Paris as Titania,
and Bernard Bresslaw as Bottom, in Regent's Park Open Air Theatre's
1980 production of *A Midsummer Night's Dream*.

To Sophie

Oxford School Shakespeare
edited by Roma Gill

A Midsummer Night's Dream
Romeo and Juliet
As You Like It
Macbeth
Julius Caesar
The Merchant of Venice
Henry IV Part 1
Twelfth Night
The Taming of the Shrew
Othello
Hamlet
King Lear
Henry V
The Winter's Tale
Antony and Cleopatra
The Tempest

Printed in the United Kingdom at the University Press, Cambridge

Contents

A great occasion

Think of a wedding—a very special wedding, because the bridegroom is a most important person. He is of noble birth, and for many years his family has owned the land for miles around their stately home. He is a good landlord—his tenants, the workmen living on his estate, love him and share in the rejoicing at his marriage. As a kind of wedding-present they have rehearsed a play to entertain the guests when the religious ceremonies are completed and the feasting is over.

The paragraph you have just read is not intended as a summary of the action of *A Midsummer Night's Dream*. It is a simple description of *any* great wedding in Elizabethan England; many are reported in the chronicles of the time.

But one particular wedding must have been very grand. The guest of honour (almost more important than the bride and bridegroom) was the Queen herself, Her Majesty Elizabeth I of England. And the entertainment was provided not by well-meaning amateurs, but by a company of professional actors. The play they performed had been written especially for this occasion by the best dramatist of the time—Mr William Shakespeare.

What kind of entertainment would be *right* for this very special occasion? Nothing solemn or serious—the audience is relaxed and happy. Not a critical satire: wedding guests have not come to hear an intellectual debate. Something romantic—and at the same time comic; with poetry—songs—dances; with speeches in praise of married love—and also (because the Virgin Queen is to be present) in praise of chastity and the single life. And perhaps a little touch of magic—because for the two people most intimately concerned, the bride and bridegroom, their wedding is a mystical event, which must be celebrated with proper ceremony.

I'm sure that Shakespeare did not sit down and make such a list of ingredients! Writing a play is not a mechanical act, but a work of imagination; and Shakespeare's mind was never more actively imaginative than when he created *A Midsummer Night's Dream*. But the 'ingredients' that I have listed are all present in the play (and there are many more besides). All are calculated to charm, honour, amuse, and arouse the sympathies of two noble Elizabethan families, assembled with their friends and their Queen to witness the marriage of two young people.

Afterwards, *A Midsummer Night's Dream* became the property of the theatrical company for which Shakespeare was the leading dramatist. It was performed in public theatres at the end of the sixteenth century, and it has delighted audiences ever since. It was a favourite in the nineteenth century, when it was produced in London *with real rabbits*. Parts of the plot have been used for ballet and opera, and the play has inspired great painters and musicians. Mendelssohn's 'Wedding March', first written in the early nineteenth century to introduce Act 5, is still the most popular music played at English weddings when the newly-married couple walk out of the church together.

A Midsummer Night's Dream is not like any of Shakespeare's other plays; this is why I want you to think about the circumstances in which it was first performed. Shakespeare is famous for creating characters who are so convincing that they sometimes seem more real than the people in ordinary life. For centuries readers and audiences have argued about the Prince of Denmark, the hero of the play *Hamlet*. Is this man good or bad? Should he have revenged his father's death, or not? But in *A Midsummer Night's Dream* the characters are simple to understand, and there is no doubt why each one acts as he or she does. And the play does not really have a main plot—unlike the other thirty-six plays that Shakespeare wrote. There are three stories, or 'actions', in this play.

a) a love story, showing the changing relationships between four young people;
b) a comic account of amateur actors struggling to rehearse and perform a very bad play;
c) a fairy story, in which the king of the fairies quarrels with his queen, punishes her, and then forgives her.

These three actions are almost entirely separate from each other, and the characters concerned in one story usually do not know anything about the other stories. Yet all three actions, and the characters belonging to them, are connected: but the threads that tie them together are very delicate.

In *A Midsummer Night's Dream* Shakespeare is offering (instead of his usual strong plots and profound character-studies) a wide variety of entertainment, ranging from uproarious comedy to a serious account of the nature of poetic imagination. The different elements are linked together and unified by the theme that runs through the play. It is a most appropriate theme for the occasion: love and marriage.

Characters in the play

Before their stories begin, I think it will be helpful to look at the characters whom Shakespeare has brought together into this play. There are three stories—and *four* sets of characters.

1. Theseus and Hippolyta

These two figures are from Greek mythology. Theseus was the son of a legendary king of Athens, closely related to Hercules, the Greek super-man. There are many narratives which tell how Theseus fought with monsters; how he killed the Minotaur that threatened to destroy the island of Crete; how princesses fell in love with him; and how he defeated an invasion of Amazons and married their queen, Hippolyta.

From time to time during the course of *A Midsummer Night's Dream* Shakespeare refers to the myths, re-creating Theseus as an almost-historical being.

The Amazons were a nation of women-warriors, who despised men and refused to marry. It was thought that they came originally from Africa, and that they conquered almost the whole of Asia before being defeated by Theseus. *A Midsummer Night's Dream* begins just a few days before the marriage of Theseus and Hippolyta, and the play ends on the night of the wedding. Nothing *happens* to the two legendary figures, but their marriage provides Shakespeare with a kind of framework for the stories of his own invention.

2. The lovers

Hermia and Helena
Lysander and Demetrius

These are creatures of Shakespeare's imagination, although he took their names from the classical traditions that gave him the persons of Theseus and Hippolyta. Because the lovers are Athenians from classical Greece, they worship the gods of Greek mythology. Hermia is prepared to become a nun in the service of Diana, goddess of chastity; and Helena blames Cupid, the mischievous god of love, for all her misfortunes.

But these lovers are not figures from the dim and distant past. Hermia is a hot-tempered young woman who is very conscious of the fact that she is smaller than Helena, and rather jealous of her friend's fair-haired beauty. And Helena, tall and blonde, suffers agonies of love for the man (Demetrius) who once promised to marry her and who has now fallen in love with Hermia. Demetrius is only distinguished from his rival Lysander by being much more competitive. He wants to win Hermia's hand in marriage (although she says she does not love him), and he constantly tries to impress everyone (especially Theseus) with his witty comments.

3. The workmen

Often, when these comedy characters are mentioned in the play, we are reminded that they too are Greek: 'Hard-handed men that work in Athens here' (5, 1, 72). But we ignore the reminder. The amateur actors are essentially sixteenth-century Englishmen, whose names declare their occupations:

Quince — the carpenter: his name is taken from the 'quoins'—wedge-shaped pieces of wood used in building.

Snug — the joiner, who must make the pieces of wood fit snugly together.

Snout — the tinker, whose regular job it was to repair the snouts—spouts— of kettles.

Bottom — the weaver, so called because in weaving the thread is wound on a reel or 'bottom'.

Flute — the bellows-maker; a whistling sound is produced when bellows are squeezed to blow air either on to coals (to make the fire burn) or into church organ-pipes.

Starveling — the tailor, who owes his name to the popular belief that tailors were always very thin.

Although they are called 'rude mechanicals' (3,2,9), we must not assume that these men have had no education. Snug, obviously, was not very bright at his lessons: he confesses that he is 'slow of study' (1,2,63). But Elizabethan tradesmen certainly sent their sons to school, and this is perhaps where Bottom learned the long words that he is so proud to use (although he is not very sure of their meanings). Peter Quince is the most intelligent of workmen. He can correct mispronunciations and misunderstandings, and he knows about the fables of classical mythology. He would certainly have learned this at an Elizabethan grammar school.

When these characters wish to express themselves emphatically, or utter a mild oath, they do not call upon the classical gods. Instead they swear 'By'r lakin' or 'Marry'—invoking the Virgin Mary and showing that they belong to a Christian tradition.

4. The fairies

Every community has its own superstitions concerning beings that are neither human (although they may appear in human form) nor divine. These are immortal, and usually ageless. They possess some magical powers, and they can use these either to assist mortals or to annoy them. The beliefs vary from one nation to another; within the British Isles ideas about fairies vary from county to county. Often one small village cannot agree with its nearest neighbour about the invisible creatures that live in the nearby woods, or underneath the hill, or at the bottom of the garden. It is not surprising that Shakespeare knew a lot about supernatural beings and their activities. As a boy he lived in a small market-town, and fairy stories are much more common in the country than in cities. In addition, he read widely, learning from books about the more *literary* types of fairy. The human characters in *A Midsummer Night's Dream* come from at least two different worlds—the world of classical mythology and the everyday world of Elizabethan England. And the fairies, too, belong to different traditions.

Titania is the fairy with the longest history. The Roman poet Ovid gives this name to Diana, goddess of chastity. Shakespeare's fairy queen is certainly not a goddess, but there are some similarities between Titania and the pagan deities. Early in the play Titania speaks (2,1,123ff) of having women followers (like an order of nuns) who devote themselves to her service. Most importantly, she is convinced that her quarrels with Oberon have caused havoc in the lives of the 'human mortals': the fairies have neglected the proper ceremonials, and as a result the elements—wind, rain, and sun—have been disturbed (2,1,82ff). Titania is, however, quite unlike the classical goddess of chastity, because she is married to Oberon.

Oberon Titania's husband first appears as king of the fairies in a French romance written in the fifteenth century and translated into English shortly before Shakespeare wrote his play.

Shakespeare gives Oberon a wife, and he also suggests that, like Titania, Oberon belongs to the period of classical myth. Titania accuses Oberon of being in love with Hippolyta; and Oberon in turn accuses his wife of giving too much assistance to Theseus (2,1,76ff). There is no 'truth' in these mutual accusations, of course; as Titania says, they are 'the forgeries of jealousy' (2,1,81).

In the play, however, these 'forgeries' serve two useful purposes. It is common for husbands and wives to taunt each other about past love affairs, and this quarrel makes Oberon and Titania seem much more real. Also, because we recognize Hippolyta and Theseus as full-sized human beings, we are encouraged to think of the fairy king and queen in the same dimensions. Shakespeare does *not* want us to do this with the other fairies who are their attendants and courtiers.

Peaseblossom
Cobweb
Moth
Mustardseed

Only four of the fairy attendants have names, but as we read we imagine that there are many more than four of these tiny creatures. Certainly one nameless fairy has a 'speaking part', and it is he (or perhaps she) who first describes fairy forms and activities. We are told (in *Act 2*, scene 1) that the fairies are very small: compared to them cowslips are 'tall', and acorn-cups make safe hiding-places. The four names suggest that their owners are not only tiny but also very fragile: a cobweb is easily brushed aside, and moths must be handled very delicately.

Shakespeare had no source for these fairies except his own invention. English children today recognize them easily, but they were quite unknown before *A Midsummer Night's Dream* was written. When narratives composed earlier than this play tell of 'fairies' they refer to quite different creatures who are the size of human beings and usually hostile to mortals. A particularly unpleasant trait of these 'old style' fairies was their habit of stealing beautiful human children from their cradles, and substituting weak or ugly fairy children. The babies who were exchanged in this way were known as 'changelings'—and this practice is alluded to in *Act 2*, scene 1.

Shakespeare's fairies, however, care for human beings. They also (we are told) look after the wild flowers in the woods. But their chief occupation is dancing, usually in a formal circle, and it seems as though this activity casts some kind of spell, making the place safe and even holy. Oberon explains carefully that he and the fairies of his court are not evil spirits, like the ghosts of damned souls who can only appear during the hours of darkness (*3,2,388ff*). Yet the fairies are particularly associated with night, and they are most awake when mortals are asleep.

 Puck

Probably the most famous of all Shakespeare's fairy characters is Puck—but Puck is not the product of the dramatist's own imagination. Until Shakespeare wrote *A Midsummer Night's Dream* it was possible to speak of *a* puck, or *the* puck. A puck was simply a *kind* of fairy, and stories about pucks are common throughout the British Isles. They were mischievous beings, able to change their shapes into human or animal forms, and especially

likely to appear as flickering lights to mislead travellers in the
night. At heart, however, the puck was a friendly spirit—
and sometimes called 'Robin Goodfellow': he was sympathetic
to mortals who spoke politely to him: kind to lovers; and always
ready to help the housewife who tried to keep her home
clean and tidy. Shakespeare refers to many of the qualities that
tradition attributes to the puck, and he places this fairy at the
centre of his play. Puck is given an official position in the fairy
court, where his job is to 'jest to Oberon, and make him smile'
(2,1,44). He is Oberon's agent when the king of the fairies tries to
help the human lovers; and it is he who is responsible for all the
complications that arise in the play.

Perhaps it is also Puck who expresses the feelings of the
audience when he contemplates the situation and remarks, with
gentle amusement, 'Lord what fools these mortals be' (3,2,115).

A Midsummer Night's Dream

A Midsummer Night's Dream begins and ends in Athens. Here is Theseus's palace, and the home of Peter Quince. It is a civilized society in which every man knows his place, from the duke (whose function it is to administer law and justice) to the humblest workman (who must take care not to offend the ladies). This is where we first meet the human characters. Theseus and Hippolyta are eagerly awaiting their wedding-day; the lovers have already got their relationships in a tangle; and the workmen have started a project far more adventurous than anything they have undertaken before.

Theseus and Hippolyta remain in Athens whilst we (as audience or readers) accompany the lovers and the workmen on their *separate* expeditions outside the city walls, into the forest that surrounds Athens.

The forest belongs to the fairies: Athenian law does not operate here. Oberon tries to impose some kind of rule, but he is not a god and he makes mistakes. The first scene in the forest shows us the fairies at their best and at their worst. At their best they are caring for the wild flowers; at their worst they are quarrelling furiously, and their quarrels have serious repercussions in the lives of human beings.

The lovers and the workmen enter the fairy realm and soon become aware of the strangeness of their surroundings. It is a strangeness that grows frightening as night approaches.

Shakespeare is not precise about the length of time that the humans spend in the woods. The first forest scene is brightly lit: Oberon greets his wife with the words 'Ill met by moonlight, proud Titania' (2,1,60). But the night (if it is the *same* night) seems to grow darker. There are mistakes and misunderstandings. The mortals are all lost: they cannot find the way out of their own problems, or out of the wood. The workmen managed to escape (with some damage to their clothing), but the lovers are separated in the darkness and eventually lie down to sleep feeling alone and afraid. In fact they are all together, and perfectly safe.

The time spent in the forest is the period immediately before Theseus's wedding, and that has been arranged so that

> the moon, like to a silver bow
> New-bent in heaven, shall behold the night
> Of our solemnities   (*1*,1,9-11)

Before a new moon is seen, the only night light comes from the stars.

Although the night is dark, it is very short—the shortest night of the year: the play's title tells us this. In England, and in most European countries, the night before midsummer day has always been associated with magic, fairies, and lovers. It is also a time for madness. The phrase 'midsummer madness' is still used to describe a state of mind which is abnormal (perhaps affected by the heat of the sun—or by fairy power) but which does not last long.

Light dawns when Theseus and Hippolyta come out of the city in order to pay some kind of homage to the midsummer season. Slowly the lovers recover from their temporary 'madness'—and we all return to Athens and ordered civilization.

The play ends with three weddings—a triple celebration of this civilization. Without an ordered society, marriage is impossible; and every wedding—every permanent bond between two people—strengthens the society in which it occurs.

Finally it is the turn of the fairies to enter 'foreign' territory: they come from the wood to the palace in order to bless the three marriages within the play. But there is a sense in which this fairy blessing is not bestowed only on Theseus, Hippolyta, and the other four lovers. When Oberon says 'To the best bride-bed will we' (5,1,390) he is surely referring not to the characters assembled on the stage, but to the main personages seated in the audience—the bride and bridegroom, in whose honour this play has been performed.

The Lovers' story

Act I

Scene 1   It is Lysander who first decides to leave Athens. He is in love with Hermia, and she loves him. But her father has ordered Hermia to marry another man, Demetrius, and 'the sharp Athenian law' is such that disobedience may be punished by death. Not even the duke can alter the law—although he is able to offer another alternative: she can become a nun.

Theseus speaks in praise of those who 'master so their blood' and 'undergo such maiden pilgrimage'—those who chose (as Queen Elizabeth I did) to live without husband or children in order to dedicate their lives wholly to some service. His words, however, stress the harshness of this single life: it is 'cold', 'fruitless', 'barren' and restricted. Theseus, we must not forget, is about to be a bridegroom himself.

Hermia is firm in her decision, and she earns our respect for her loyalty to Lysander, despite the threats of her father and the persuasions of the duke. We become still more sympathetic to her when we learn that Demetrius, the man her father prefers, has been courting another sweetheart.

As soon as we understand the situation perfectly, all the characters follow the duke from the stage, leaving only Lysander and Hermia. Lysander is worried, and Hermia is almost in tears— but for about twenty lines Shakespeare holds up the action, whilst the two lovers deliver a dialogue on the subject of love and its problems. We must react to these lines in two ways, simultaneously. On one level we understand that the characters are consoling each other by remembering that lovers have always had problems. At the same time, our attention is drawn not to *what* is said, but to *how* it is being said. These lines are very clever, but they are not at all naturalistic. In real life people do not speak like this:

Lysander
The course of true love never did run smooth;
But either it was different in blood—

Hermia

O cross! too high to be enthrall'd to low.

Lysander

Or else misgraffed in respect of years—

Hermia

O spite! too old to be engag'd to young . . .

The technique is a skilful one. Hermia's situation could be very serious: a matter of life or death. Shakespeare wants us to sympathize with the dilemma—but he does not wish his audience to be anxious. The artificial, 'patterned' verse serves to remind us that this is a play—a comedy, in fact—and that no-one is in serious danger. We can wonder how things will work out; but we can be sure that the ending will be a happy one.

After we have heard Lysander's plot to escape from Athens, we meet the fourth of the set of lovers. We already know that Helena is desperately in love with Demetrius—that she 'dotes, Devoutly dotes, dotes in idolatry' upon him. In every way Helena is the exact opposite of Hermia: later in a reading of the play we learn that Hermia is small and dark, whilst Helena is tall and fair. This is, of course, immediately apparent when the play is performed. The different physical characteristics emphasize the different personalities: Hermia is quick, hot-tempered and energetic, whilst Helena is languid and almost seems to be *enjoying* her misery!

Act 2

Scene 1   This is still our impression when we see Helena a second time, after she has betrayed her friend's secret and followed Demetrius into the forest in pursuit of the runaway lovers. Demetrius does not appear as a very attractive character when he insults Helena and threatens her; but she invites such treatment:

I am your spaniel; and, Demetrius,
The more you beat me, I will fawn on you:
Use me but as your spaniel, spurn me, strike me . . .

Demetrius warns Helena of the potential danger:

You do impeach your modesty too much,
To leave the city, and commit yourself
Into the hands of one that loves you not.

His words are threatening, and the situation looks dangerous—but once again we are not alarmed. Before Demetrius and Helena rushed on to the stage, Oberon stood there alone. The fairy king did not leave the stage when he heard the approach of the mortals. He stepped aside, perhaps throwing a dark cloak around himself, and informed the audience

> I am invisible,
> And I will overhear their conference

The presence of Oberon is enough protection for Helena; although she cannot see him, he is in full view of the audience; and as readers we must try to 'see' the scene with a dramatic imagination.

The slight hint of danger is completely dispelled when Helena replies to Demetrius's warnings: *she* threatens *him*—and he is the one who runs away!

When Oberon decides to intervene in the lovers' dispute, and instructs Puck to search for Demetrius, we know exactly what will happen. Oberon tells Puck 'Thou shalt know the man By the Athenian garments he hath on'. *We* know—but Oberon and Puck do not—that there are two Athenians in the forest; and we can be sure that identities will be mistaken.

Scene 2 The arrival of Lysander and Hermia encourages our expectations. They are tired, and lost. We are sympathetic—yet we also smile. Once again it is the form of the verse that relaxes tension. This time the lines are rhymed couplets; and to emphasize the artificiality there are double meanings which the lovers work out for their own pleasure, taking delight in the skill of their language—so much so that Hermia even compliments her lover: 'Lysander riddles very prettily'. When Demetrius and Helena rush back on to the stage, they too speak in rhymed couplets—and the effect of this is comparable with the effects of an English Christmas pantomime. The action is too fast for serious emotion. It is halted for a moment by Helena's lament after Demetrius has left her, but the pause only gives the audience time to enjoy a delightful suspense. We have been told of the effects of the love-juice; we know that it has been sprinkled on the *wrong* Athenian's eyes; and we wait for Helena's discovery:

> But who is here? Lysander! on the ground!
> Dead? or asleep? I see no blood, no wound.
> Lysander, if you live, good sir, awake.

Lysander's reaction is prompt:

And run through fire I will for thy sweet sake.

Nothing can follow this rhyme except laughter.

Lysander now courts Helena with exaggerated protestations of love. Helena believes that he is making fun of her, and runs away. Lysander turns on the sleeping Hermia, showing a surprising hatred. And Hermia wakes from a terrifying dream, to find herself alone and lost in the wood.

Act 3

Scene 2   Oberon, trying to remedy Puck's mistake, succeeds only in adding to the confusion when he anoints Demetrius's eyes with the love-juice so that he too falls in love with Helena. Demetrius declares his passion with extravagant praise of Helena's beauty:

O Helen, goddess, nymph, perfect, divine!
To what, my love, shall I compare thine eyne?
Crystal is muddy. O how ripe in show
Thy lips, those kissing cherries, tempting grow.

The poetry is intentionally bad; and it is no wonder that Helena believes she is being mocked. For a time we see the situation as it must appear to Puck—and enjoy the comedy as much as he does:

Then will two at once woo one;
That must needs be sport alone;
And those things do best please me
That befall preposterously.

When Hermia joins the other three lovers (also speaking in their rhymed couplets) the comedy continues for a short time, and then the mood of the scene becomes more serious. The signal for this change of mood is in the verse, which suddenly loses its rhymes and begins to sound more like ordinary speech, allowing Helena and Hermia to engage in a bitter quarrel.

Helena's description of the schooldays she shared with Hermia is very pretty—and extremely sentimental. She is nostalgic, longing for the relationship which she claims to have had with Hermia and which she feels has been betrayed by her friend's conduct:

The Actors' story

Act 1

In the first scene of *A Midsummer Night's Dream* we are introduced to the lovers and their very tense emotional situation. It is a scene of high passions: a father demands his daughter's obedience and threatens her with death; the daughter is resolved to marry the man she loves; rival suitors threaten each other; and a hopeless Helena laments for her unfaithful lover. These passions are all expressed in verse—verse which at different times (and for different reasons) becomes highly 'poetic' and obviously 'pattern-ed'. The scene that follows this is in complete contrast, and the contrast is immediately marked by the change from verse to plain, straightforward prose.

Scene 2 The only conflict in Scene 2 is the struggle for power between Peter Quince and Nick Bottom. Quince tries, with all the tact he can command, to control his would-be actors. Bottom wants to cast himself in every available part, so that he can act not only Pyramus and Thisbe, but also the lion.

By taking a roll-call of his actors, calling them 'man by man according to the scrip', Peter Quince introduces the individual members of his company; we learn their names and occupations. It is Bottom that we are most interested in, and it is important that his character is firmly established in this scene.

The play chosen to entertain Theseus 'on his wedding-day at night' is Shakespeare's parody of much minor drama that was written in the sixteenth century, and which was often presented on just such occasions. Quince refers to it as an 'interlude', and this is the correct technical term for the diversion performed *between* (Latin *inter* = between) the different events on a formal occasion. In the last scene of the play Theseus asks for some amusement

> To wear away this long age of three hours
> Between our after-supper and bed-time.   (5,1,33–4)

And will you rent our ancient love asunder,
To join with men in scorning your poor friend?

But when Hermia refuses to share her nostalgia, Helena begins to lose her temper—and we are given a very different picture of the early friendship:

O, when she's angry, she is keen and shrewd.
She was a vixen when she went to school.

The quarrel between the 'painted maypole', Helena, and the 'puppet', Hermia, is intense; but it does not last long. Oberon and Puck are always visible (to the audience) and when the bewildered men and the angry girls leave the stage we are reassured that all will be well. The harmony is restored through the magical rhymes of Oberon and Puck.

Under his master's instructions Puck takes command of the situation. Some of the time he behaves like the fairy spirit—the puck—after whom he is named: he misleads Lysander and Demetrius, imitating their voices until they are confused and utterly lost. At other times he is calm and sensible—and rather amused by the work he has to do. He is like a busy stage-manager—or a teacher—efficiently assembling his charges:

Yet but three? Come one more;
Two of both kinds makes up four.
Here she comes, curst and sad:
Cupid is a knavish lad,
Thus to make poor females mad.

Act 4

Scene 1   Now the lovers can sleep in safety until they are woken by the arrival of the hunting-party from the palace. As they follow Theseus back to Athens they try to recall and explain the events of the night but, like dreams, these quickly fade from the memory.

Many interludes were based on stories from classical mythology, because this was the Elizabethans' favourite kind of light reading—but Shakespeare enjoys the comedy that inevitably arises when simple working men try to deal with sophisticated fictions.

Act 3

Scene 1   When the workmen meet in the forest for their first rehearsal they have had time to think about their play—especially about the practical difficulties of staging this entertainment in the great hall of the palace. They have both too much, and too little, imagination; and they assume that their audience will think as they themselves do. The lion presents a serious problem:

Will not the ladies be afeard of the lion?

Shakespeare's first audience would have known that this problem had arisen in a similar production only two years earlier, at a christening party in the Scottish court. The plan there was to have a chariot drawn by a *real* lion—but the plan had been abandoned in the interests of the spectators' safety.

Having sorted out their difficulties, the actors begin to rehearse—with Puck as an unseen audience. But their rehearsal is interrupted when the leading actor—Bottom—is transformed into a monster by Puck's trickery. The workmen hurry back to Athens in panic, and we see no more of them until we too are taken back inside the city walls.

Act 4

Scene 2   Here they are naturally very depressed, grieving over the loss of Bottom. They are quite sure that the duke would have rewarded Bottom's acting talent by making him an official servant, with a pension of 'sixpence a day during life'. Shakespeare's acting company had this kind of official status, with the patronage of the Lord Chamberlain at first and later (after 1603) of King James I.

The audience, however, knows what has happened to Bottom. His adventure with the fairy queen was strange but (like a dream) it is quickly fading from his memory. When Puck released Bottom (in *Act 4*, scene 1) and sent him back to his friends, Bottom tried desperately to explain to himself what had happened. He struggled to find words:

> Methought I was—there is no man can tell what. Methought I was—and methought I had—but man is but a patched fool if he will offer to say what methought I had.

When he rushes back to his fellow-actors he has almost completely forgotten the episode. He promises 'to discourse wonders', but for the moment it is more important to hurry the other actors along to the palace, to present their play.

Act 5

Scene 1   In the programme which is offered to Theseus the play of 'Pyramus and Thisbe' is described as 'A tedious brief scene' which offers 'very tragical mirth'. Naturally, Theseus finds this description intriguing, but his pompous master-of-ceremonies, Philostrate, sneers at the play and despises the actors, 'Which never labour'd in their minds till now'. He tries to persuade Theseus not to choose this play—but Theseus is a generous ruler. He understands that the play is being offered by the workmen in 'simpleness and duty'; and he also understands that it is *his* duty to acccept the gift graciously. As he explains his attitude to Hippolita he resembles Queen Elizabeth I, who is often praised by the sixteenth-century chroniclers for her graciousness in accepting the well-meant tributes of her subjects (which unkind observers—like Demetrius—might find comic).

When Quince reads the Prologue we become aware of what a very great occasion this is for him and the other 'rude mechanicals'. At first he stumbles badly over the punctuation—but when he is joined by the other actors he seems to get a little more confidence. In productions of this kind it was quite normal to have an account of the play read out (as Quince now reads) before the action starts—but Shakespeare obviously thought that this was old-fashioned and unnecessary, and he makes good comic use out of the convention.

When Snout, Snug, and Starveling speak, explaining their parts in the play (as Wall, Lion and Moonshine) we remember the problems that were raised at the forest rehearsal. This is how they have been coped with. How much imagination should one bring—either as an actor or as a member of the audience—to a dramatic performance? Snout explains far too much: perhaps he could have been accepted as 'Wall' when he first entered, but by the time he has finished speaking he is unmistakably Snout the tinker. The same is true of Snug and Starveling—and indeed the latter becomes so impatient with the audience's fault-finding that he speaks to them in his own workman's prose:

> All I have to say is to tell you that the lantern is the moon; I, the man in the moon; this thorn-bush, my thorn-bush; and this dog, my dog.

Bottom as Pyramus makes his assignation with Thisbe (mispronouncing a few classical names as he does so). His great moment, however, is the discovery of Thisbe's torn mantle: he stabs himself and dies. The dying is a very long process, allowing him time to lament his cruel fate, to praise Thisbe's beauty, to curse the lion, and to announce the fact of his own death:

> Now am I dead,
> Now am I fled;
> My soul is in the sky.

He orders the moon to depart—and Starveling is obedient:

> Tongue lose thy light!
> Moon, take thy flight!
> Now die, die, die, die, die.

At last he is silent; and there is time for Thisbe's speech in praise of her dead lover. For Flute (as for Bottom) the rhymes are more important than the sense of the words:

> These lily lips,
> This cherry nose,
> These yellow cowslip cheeks,
> Are gone, are gone:
> Lovers make moan!
> His eyes were green as leeks.

Thisbe too dies with considerable style—and, as Theseus observes, 'Moonshine and Lion are left to bury the dead'.

The play has served its function for the Athenian wedding-party: it 'hath well beguil'd The heavy gait of night', and the courtiers can retire to bed.

The Fairies' story

Act 2

Scene 1   The conflict between Oberon and Titania can easily be expressed
in human terms, but the effects of the conflict are supernatural and
it can only be resolved by magic.

   The basis of the quarrel is the refusal of a mother (in fact, a
foster-mother) to allow her child to grow up. Titania has adopted
the Indian boy whose mother served her, but now Oberon feels
that it is time for the child to become one of his attendants—
'Knight of his train, to trace the forest wild'. The fairy king and
queen have been quarrelling for a long time over this very human
matter.

   Quarrels between supernatural beings, however, have serious
consequences. The seasons of the year have got mixed up—
harvests are ruined by rain, and roses bloom in winter. The climate
is wet and cold, so that 'rheumatic diseases do abound'. Human
beings are suffering, and Titania is sorry for them. Oberon too
feels some sympathy—but he will not give way to Titania's wishes.

   He calls upon the magical powers of the herb 'love-in-
idleness', and in one of the most beautiful passages in the play he
describes exactly how the herb acquired its power: the myth is
Shakespeare's own creation. Cupid, the god of love, shot one of his
arrows at 'a fair vestal throned by the west'; but the woman's
chastity and devotion to her duty were so strong that Cupid's
arrow had no effect. It fell harmlessly to earth, whilst the woman
(who of course was Elizabeth I) proceeded through life 'In maiden
meditation, fancy-free'. Oberon, however, was able to see where
Cupid's arrow had fallen—upon 'a little western flower' that was
once white but then became 'purple with love's wound'. It is this
that he uses with such devastating effect upon the eyes of
Demetrius and Lysander, as well as those of Titania.

Act 3

Scene 1   The herb has the power to 'make or man or woman madly dote
Upon the next live creature that it sees'. By sheer good luck (or
good dramatic management) Puck is able to place Bottom, with the
ass-head on his shoulders, immediately before the waking Titania.
Titania duly falls in love with Bottom who, despite the ass-head,
remains essentially the Athenian workman—the character established for him in *Act 1*, scene 2. He is fully in control of the
situation in which he finds himself; he expresses no surprise at the
fairy attendants, and he is smugly satisfied at his ability to
command them. Even Titania's love does not surprise him. She
prettily declares her passion for him, using very poetic language:

> I pray thee, gentle mortal, sing again!
> Mine ear is much enamour'd of thy note;
> So is mine eye enthralled to thy shape;
> And thy fair virtue's force perforce doth move me
> On the first view to say, to swear, I love thee.

Bottom accepts her love. And he speaks to Titania just as he would
address a woman of his own rank—in plain straightforward prose:

> Methinks, mistress, you should have little reason for that.
> And yet, to say the truth, reason and love keep little company
> together nowadays.

Of course, when Titania's eyes have been released from the spell,
she is horrified to see what she has done. She repents of her quarrel
with Oberon, and gladly gives him the Indian boy.

Act 5

Scene 1   Oberon and Titania are happy and united, prepared for their final
appearance in the play—to pronounce the benediction on the
human weddings. Perhaps the first performance ended with this
fairy blessing:

> With this field-dew consecrate,
> Every fairy take his gait,
> And each several chamber bless,
> Through this palace, with sweet peace;
> And the owner of it blest,
> Ever shall in safety rest.

Synopsis

Act 1   *Athens*

Scene 1   Theseus and Hippolyta are longing for their wedding-day. Egeus demands that his daughter, Hermia, should be forced to marry Demetrius. Hermia decides to escape from Athens with her lover, Lysander. They confide in Helena; and she goes to tell Demetrius of their plans.

Scene 2   Peter Quince chooses the cast for his play.

Act 2   *The Forest*

Scene 1   Oberon and Titania are quarrelling. Oberon sends Puck to find the love-juice. Demetrius has come into the forest in pursuit of Hermia, and Helena has followed him. She pleads for his love. Oberon takes pity on her, and orders Puck to put some of the love-juice on the Athenian lover's eyes. He himself goes to use it on Titania.

Scene 2   Whilst Titania is sleeping, Oberon anoints her eyes with the magic juice. Hermia and Lysander lie down to sleep, and Puck mistakenly squeezes the love-juice on to the *wrong* Athenian's eyes. When Helena enters, Lysander awakes and falls in love with her. He follows Helena, leaving Hermia to wake up alone.

Act 3   *The Forest*

Scene 1   The actors meet to rehearse their play. Puck fits the 'ass-head' over Bottom's head. Titania wakes, and falls in love with Bottom.

Scene 2   Puck reports his trick to Oberon, but they both learn how he has mistaken the lovers when Demetrius comes with Hermia, still pleading for his love. She leaves him, and he falls asleep. Oberon tries to remedy Puck's mistake by squeezing the love-juice on to Demetrius's eyes. Puck is sent to fetch Helena. Demetrius wakes, and declares his love to Helena — who now thinks that both the men are making fun of her. Hermia returns. The two girls begin to quarrel, and the men are ready to fight each other. But Oberon sends Puck to separate them. They all get lost in a dark mist; and each one lies down to sleep. Puck removes the charm from Lysander's eyes.

Act 4   *The Forest*

Scene 1   Titania plays with Bottom and her fairies until she falls asleep. Oberon watches her for a time; then he feels sorry for Titania and takes the charm off her eyes. She wakes up, and looks on Bottom with horror. Theseus, out hunting, discovers the four sleeping lovers. When they awake, they follow him back to the court. Finally Bottom wakes up, and goes home to find his friends.

Scene 2   Back in Athens, Bottom rejoins the other actors.

Act 5   *Athens*

Scene 1   Theseus chooses the evening's entertainment. Peter Quince's company perform their play. The lovers all go to bed, and the fairies come to give a blessing to the marriages.

'of imagination all compact'

The magic certainly ends when Oberon and Titania leave the stage. Puck, with his broom and epilogue, introduces a down-to-earth note. He speaks directly to the audience, suggesting that they too, like the lovers and Bottom, have been asleep: 'you have but slumber'd here'. All the strange things that they have witnessed have been 'No more yielding but a dream'.

Puck speaks of 'shadows', and at first it seems that he is referring to the other fairies. But in fact he is speaking on behalf of all the actors who have taken part in *A Midsummer Night's Dream*. Shakespeare often (in his other plays) calls actors 'shadows', and in Act 5 of this play we can almost hear Shakespeare speaking through Theseus when the duke, referring to the amateur actors of 'Pyramus and Thisbe', says

> The best in this kind are but shadows, and the worst are no worse, if imagination amend them.

Shakespeare felt that actors have no substance or identity in themselves. They exist in order to lend their bodies and their talents to the personalities of the play. Whilst the play is being performed, only the characters—Theseus, Titania, Bottom, Hermia and the rest—are important.

The spectators have agreed—by coming to watch the performance—to share in the dramatist's imagination; and to bring along *their own* imaginations to supply anything that is lacking in the production. So when Oberon says 'Ill met by moonlight, proud Titania', the audience must be prepared to believe that the moon is shining—even though the performance takes place in broad daylight. This is something that the workmen cannot comprehend:

> **Quince**
> But there is two hard things: that is, to bring the moonlight into a chamber; for, you know, Pyramus and Thisbe meet by moonlight.
> **Snout**
> Doth the moon shine that night we play our play?

Bottom

A calendar, a calendar! Look in the almanac; find out moonshine, find out moonshine.

Theseus says that imagination will improve—'amend'—the mechanicals' performance, and Hippolita points out that 'It must be your imagination then, and not theirs'.

At the beginning of Act 5 Theseus explains how the poet's imagination works; this is surely Shakespeare's account of his own 'shaping fantasies'. The poet is 'of imagination all compact', and his imagination 'bodies forth The forms of things unknown'. Perfect examples of this are the tiny fairies, Peaseblossom, Cobweb, Moth and Mustardseed, who were totally unknown until Shakespeare wrote this play. His pen has 'Turn[ed] them to shapes' and given 'to airy nothing A local habitation and a name'.

Theseus tells us that the poet is first of all an observer, and that his eyes survey the whole of his universe—'from heaven to earth, from earth to heaven'. This gives him his material: most of the time he does not invent from nothing. In this play we can see how Shakespeare has read classical mythology, and French narrative fiction; how he is well-informed about folk-lore; and how he has watched the workmen of his own town and time. Reading and observation gave him the raw materials, and then some power—imagination (aided by the craftsmanship of the experienced dramatist)—worked a kind of miracle on these 'ingredients'. And they became *A Midsummer Night's Dream*.

Shakespeare's Verse

Shakespeare's plays are mainly written in 'blank verse', the form preferred by most dramatists in the sixteenth and early seventeenth centuries. It is a very flexible medium, which is capable — like the human speaking voice — of a wide range of tones. Basically the lines, which are unrhymed, are ten syllables long. The syllables have alternating stresses, just like normal English speech; and they divide into five 'feet'. The technical name for this is 'iambic pentameter'.

> **Theseus**
> To yóu, your fáther shóuld be aś a gód;
> One that compós'd your béauties, yéa, and one
> To whóm you are but ás a fórm in wáx
> By hím imprínted, and withiń his power
> To leáve the fígure, or disfígure ít.
> Demétrius iś a worthy gentlemán.
>
> **Hermia**
> So iś Lysánder.
>
> **Theseus**
>   Iń himsélf he iś;
> But iń this kind, wantiń your fáther's voíce,
> The óther must be héld the wórthier.

1, 2, 47–55

Here the pentameter accommodates a variety of speech tones — Theseus speaks with authority when he lectures Hermia on the proper obedience of a daughter; she passionately defends her love; and Theseus replies with calm reasonableness. In this quotation the lines are all regular in length, and mostly normal in iambic stress pattern. Sometimes Shakespeare deviates from the norm, writing lines that are longer or shorter than ten syllables, and varying the stress patterns for unusual emphasis — here, Hermia's retort could be stressed 'Só is', thus reversing the iambic foot (it is now 'trochaic'). A metrical line may be divided between two — or even more — speakers, when they react quickly to each other, as Theseus is quick to respond to Hermia's objection. The verse line sometimes contains the grammatical unit of meaning — 'To you, your father should be as a god' — thereby allowing for a pause at the end of the line, before a new idea is started; at other times, the sense runs on from one line to the next — 'within his power To leave the figure, or disfigure it'. This makes for the natural fluidity of speech, avoiding monotony but still maintaining the iambic rhythm.

Date and Text

A Midsummer Night's Dream must have been in existence before 1598. The play was referred to by Francis Meres when he praised Shakespeare's work in his own book, *Palladis Tamia*. There is some other evidence that helps to fix the time of writing — most notably the Lion, the Wall, and the Wedding.

The *Lion*, which causes such a problem to the actors of 'Pyramus and Thisbe' (*Act 3*, Scene 1), was probably suggested to Shakespeare by a pamphlet published in October 1594. This described a feast in Scotland, where the scheme to bring a lion into the banqueting-hall had to be abandoned because the organizers thought that the ladies would be frightened.

The *Wall* that separates the two lovers in 'Pyramus and Thisbe' might have been something of a real problem for Shakespeare's own company when they produced his *Romeo and Juliet* (whose style is very closely linked with that of *A Midsummer Night's Dream*) in *c.* 1595.

The *Wedding* that Queen Elizabeth might have attended, and which could have been the occasion for the play, was that of Elizabeth Carey. She was the Queen's goddaughter, and both her father and her grandfather (Lord Hunsdon, the Lord Chamberlain) were patrons of Shakespeare's company.

The play was first published in 1600, and this Quarto edition — apparently printed from Shakespeare's own manuscript — is the basis of most modern texts.

Characters in the play

Theseus	*duke of Athens*
Hippolyta	*queen of the Amazons, betrothed to Theseus*
Egeus	*a nobleman, Hermia's father*
Hermia	*in love with Lysander*
Helena	*in love with Demetrius*
Lysander	
Demetrius	*young noblemen*
Philostrate	*Master of the Revels at Theseus's court*

Oberon	*king of the fairies*
Titania	*queen of the fairies*
Puck	*a mischievous fairy*
Peaseblossom	
Cobweb	
Moth	*fairies*
Mustardseed	

Peter Quince	*a carpenter*
Nick Bottom	*a weaver*
Francis Flute	*a bellows-mender*
Tom Snout	*a tinker*
Snug	*a joiner*
Robin Starveling	*a tailor*

Attendants at the court of Theseus
Fairies attending on Oberon and Titania

Hermia – marrying Demetrius loves Lysander

Helena – Best friend – loves Demetrius

Scene ①

Act I

Act I   Scene I

Theseus, who is soon to be married to Hippolyta, listens to Egeus's account of his disobedient daughter, Hermia. The girl refuses to marry Demetrius, because she is in love with Lysander. Theseus warns Hermia that she will be punished if she does not obey her father, and so Lysander and Hermia plan to run away from Athens. They tell their secret to Helena, Hermia's best friend, who is very unhappy because she is in love with Demetrius and he does not return her love.

1   *our nuptial hour :* the time of our wedding.

2   *apace :* quickly.

2–3   *four . . . moon :* there will be a new moon in four days' time.

4   *lingers :* makes me wait.

5–6   A young man could not claim full possession of his dead father's property until his mother (the 'dowager'), or his father's second wife (the 'step-dame') was also dead. Whilst the mother was growing old ('withering'), the young man's income ('revenue') would be wasting away (also 'withering').

7   *steep :* drown.

11   *solemnities :* marriage ceremonies.

12   *youth :* young people.

13   *pert :* lively.

15   We do not want unhappy (pale-faced) fellows in our festivities.

Scene I *Athens : The Palace of Theseus*

Enter Theseus, Hippolyta, Philostrate, *and* Attendants

Theseus

Now, fair Hippolyta, our nuptial hour

Draws on apace: four happy days bring in

Another moon—but O methinks, how slow

This old moon wanes! She lingers my desires,

5 Like to a step-dame or a dowager

Long withering out a young man's revenue.

Hippolyta

Four days will quickly steep themselves in night;

Four nights will quickly dream away the time;

And then the moon, like to a silver bow

10 New-bent in heaven, shall behold the night

Of our solemnities.

Theseus   Go, Philostrate,

Stir up the Athenian youth to merriments;

Awake the pert and nimble spirit of mirth;

Turn melancholy forth to funerals:

15 The pale companion is not for our pomp.

soon to be married

[*Exit* Philostrate

Hippolyta, I woo'd thee with my sword,
And won thy love doing thee injuries;
But I will wed thee in another key,
With pomp, with triumph, and with revelling.

Enter Egeus, Hermia, Lysander, *and*
Demetrius

Egeus

20 Happy be Theseus, our renowned duke!

Theseus

Thanks, good Egeus. What's the news with thee?

Egeus

Full of vexation come I, with complaint
Against my child, my daughter Hermia.
Stand forth, Demetrius. My noble lord,

25 This man hath my consent to marry her.
Stand forth, Lysander: and, my gracious duke,
This hath bewitch'd the bosom of my child:
Thou, thou, Lysander, thou hast given her rhymes,
And interchang'd love-tokens with my child;

30 Thou hast by moonlight at her window sung,
With feigning voice, verses of feigning love;
And stol'n the impression of her fantasy
With bracelets of thy hair, rings, gauds, conceits,
Knacks, trifles, nosegays, sweetmeats—messenger

35 Of strong prevailment in unharden'd youth;
With cunning hast thou filch'd my daughter's
    heart;
Turn'd her obedience, which is due to me,
To stubborn harshness. And, my gracious duke,
Be it so she will not here before your grace

40 Consent to marry with Demetrius,
I beg the ancient privilege of Athens:
As she is mine, I may dispose of her;
Which shall be either to this gentleman,
Or to her death, according to our law

45 Immediately provided in that case.

Theseus

What say you, Hermia? Be advis'd, fair maid.
To you, your father should be as a god;
One that compos'd your beauties, yea, and one
To whom you are but as a form in wax

16–17   See p. vi.
18   *another key* : a different way (the
image is from music).
19   *triumph* : public festival.

27   *bosom* : heart.
28   *rhymes* : love poetry.

31   *with feigning voice* : with a voice
that pretends to be sincere.
        feigning love : pretended love.
32   Caught her imagination by making
an impression on her.
33   *gauds* : silly toys.
        conceits : fancy things.
34   *Knacks* : knick-knacks, useless
little gifts.
        nosegays : bunches of flowers.
        sweetmeats : sweets (chocolates
would be the modern English
equivalent).
35   *prevailment* : persuasive power.
        unharden'd : inexperienced.
36   *filch'd* : stolen.
37   *due* : owed.
39   *Be it so* : if.
41   I claim the traditional right of an
Athenian.
44–5   *law . . . case* : the law specifically
designed for such cases (against which
there could be no appeal).
46   *Be advis'd* : think carefully.
49–50   *but . . . imprinted* : nothing more
than a wax figure that he has modelled.

51 *disfigure* : destroy.

(handwritten: Egeus can kill Hermia if she doesn't marry Dem)

54 *in this kind* : in a matter like this.
wanting : lacking.
voice : approval.
56 *would* : wish.

60 *concern my modesty* : affect my reputation for modesty.
61 *In such a presence* : i.e. before the duke.
plead my thoughts : express my feelings.
65 *die the death* : be legally put to death.
abjure : renounce.
67 *question your desires* : ask yourself what you really want.
68 *Know . . . youth* : remember that you are young.
blood : temperament.
69 *Whe'r* : whether.
70 *livery* : habit.
71 *aye* : ever
mew'd : shut up.
72 *sister* : nun.
73 *moon* : i.e. Diana, goddess of chastity and the moon (see p. vi.
74 *master* : discipline.
blood : passions.
75 *maiden pilgrimage* : life vowed to celibacy.
76 *earthlier happy* : more happy on earth.
the rose distill'd : the rose that is plucked, whose scent is distilled to make perfume.

50 By him imprinted, and within his power
To leave the figure or disfigure it.
Demetrius is a worthy gentleman.

Hermia
So is Lysander.

Theseus   In himself he is;

But in this kind, wanting your father's voice,
55 The other must be held the worthier.

Hermia
I would my father look'd but with my eyes.

Theseus
Rather your eyes must with his judgement look.

Hermia
I do entreat your grace to pardon me.
I know not by what power I am made bold,
60 Nor how it may concern my modesty
In such a presence here to plead my thoughts;
But I beseech your grace, that I may know
The worst that may befall me in this case,
If I refuse to wed Demetrius.

Theseus
65 Either to die the death, or to abjure
For ever the society of men.
Therefore, fair Hermia, question your desires·
Know of your youth, examine well your blood,
Whe'r, if you yield not to your father's choice,
70 You can endure the livery of a nun,
For aye to be in shady cloister mew'd,
To live a barren sister all your life,
Chanting faint hymns to the cold fruitless moon.
Thrice blessed they that master so their blood,
75 To undergo such maiden pilgrimage;
But earthlier happy is the rose distill'd,
Than that which, withering on the virgin thorn,

(handwritten: Saying not to be nun just marry Dem.)

78   *single blessedness:* celibacy. Many religions teach that a person who has vowed never to marry (to live in celibacy) is in a particular state of grace with their god.

80   Before I will surrender my right to be a virgin to the domination ('lordship') of any man whose authority I do not wish to accept.

81   *yoke:* a wooden cross-piece linking two oxen together for the purpose of ploughing; from this it becomes a symbol of bondage and servitude.

82   *give sovereignty:* acknowledge as lord and master.

83   *Take ... pause:* wait a short time before making your decision.

84   *sealing-day:* the day on which they will seal (=make official) their vows.

89   *protest:* vow.

90   *aye:* ever.
     austerity: strict simplicity. In the Christian church nuns and monks vow to live in poverty, chastity, and obedience.

92   *crazed title:* uncertain claim (because Hermia's father does not admit it).

94   *do ... him:* you go and marry him.

98   *estate unto:* give to. The phrase is a legal one, continuing the idea that Hermia is a mere possession.

99   *well deriv'd:* nobly descended, of good family.

Grows, lives, and dies, in single blessedness.
   Hermia
So will I grow, so live, so die, my lord,
80 Ere I will yield my virgin patent up
Unto his lordship, whose unwished yoke
My soul consents not to give sovereignty.
   Theseus
Take time to pause; and, by the next new moon—
The sealing-day betwixt my love and me
85 For everlasting bond of fellowship—
Upon that day either prepare to die
For disobedience to your father's will;
Or else to wed Demetrius, as he would;
Or on Diana's altar to protest
90 For aye austerity and single life.
   Demetrius
Relent, sweet Hermia; and, Lysander, yield
Thy crazed title to my certain right.
   Lysander
You have her father's love, Demetrius;
Let me have Hermia's: do you marry him.
   Egeus
95 Scornful Lysander! True, he hath my love,
And what is mine my love shall render him;
And she is mine, and all my right of her
I do estate unto Demetrius.
   Lysander
I am, my lord, as well deriv'd as he,

100 *well possess'd* : with plenty of money.
101 *fortunes* : position in life.
fairly rank'd : well esteemed.
102 *with vantage* : even better.
104 *of* : by.
105 *prosecute my right* : persist in making my claim.
106 *avouch . . . head* : declare before his face (in his presence).
107 *Made love* : courted.
108 *soul* : affections
109 *dotes in idolatry* : idolizes.
110 *spotted* : dishonourable.

113 *over-full of self-affairs* : too concerned with my own business.
114 *lose* : forget.
116 *private schooling* : advice to give you in private.
117 *For* : as for.
arm : prepare.
118 *fit . . . will* : make your wishes agree with what your father wants.
120 *extenuate* : mitigate, make easier.
122 *what cheer* : how are you feeling?
124 *business.* In modern English this word is pronounced with only two syllables; here it has three.
125 *Against* : in preparation for.
125–6 *confer . . . yourselves* : discuss something that closely concerns you.
127 *desire* : willingness.

129 *How chance* : why?

130 *Belike* : probably.
131 *Beteem* : pour down on.

132 *Ay me.* Lysander sighs.
aught : anything.

135 *different in blood* : from different social classes.

100 As well possess'd; my love is more than his;
My fortunes every way as fairly rank'd—
If not with vantage—as Demetrius';
And, which is more than all these boasts can be,
I am belov'd of beauteous Hermia.
105 Why should not I then prosecute my right?
Demetrius, I'll avouch it to his head,
Made love to Nedar's daughter, Helena,
And won her soul; and she, sweet lady, dotes,
Devoutly dotes, dotes in idolatry,
110 Upon this spotted and inconstant man.
    Theseus
I must confess that I have heard so much,
And with Demetrius thought to have spoke thereof;
But, being over-full of self-affairs,
My mind did lose it. But, Demetrius, come;
115 And come, Egeus. You shall go with me,
I have some private schooling for you both.
For you, fair Hermia, look you arm yourself
To fit your fancies to your father's will,
Or else the law of Athens yields you up—
120 Which by no means we may extenuate—
To death, or to a vow of single life.
Come, my Hippolyta: what cheer, my love?
Demetrius and Egeus, go along:
I must employ you in some business
125 Against our nuptial, and confer with you
Of something nearly that concerns yourselves.
    Egeus
With duty and desire we follow you.
    [*Exeunt all except* Lysander *and* Hermia
    Lysander
How now, my love? Why is your cheek so pale?
How chance the roses there do fade so fast?
    Hermia
130 Belike for want of rain, which I could well
Beteem them from the tempest of my eyes.
    Lysander
Ay me! For aught that I could ever read,
Could ever hear by tale or history,
The course of true love never did run smooth;
135 But, either it was different in blood—

136   What an affliction ('cross')! That a
woman should be of such high birth
that she cannot be united with a man
of lower rank.

137   *Misgraffed . . . years :* ill-matched
through difference of age.
139   *stood upon :* depended on.
friends : relations.

141   *sympathy :* agreement.
142   *lay siege to :* make war on.

145   *collied :* blackened.
146   *spleen :* sudden passionate
impulse.
unfolds : lights up.
147   *ere :* before.
149   *come to confusion :* are ruined,
destroyed.
150-51 If true lovers have always ('ever')
been frustrated ('cross'd'), there must
be some law ('edict') of fate ('destiny').
152   Let us learn to bear our suffering
('trial') with patience.
153-4 Because our suffering is a normal
('customary') frustration ('cross')
which is as much a part of being in
love as thoughts, dreams and sighs.
155   *fancy :* love.
156   *persuasion :* advice.
157-8 *dowager . . . revenue :* a widow
with a large income (from her dead
husband's estate).
159   *remote :* distant.
league : a rough measurement of
distance, usually about three miles.
160   *respects :* regards.
162-3 *the sharp . . . pursue us :* the harsh
Athenian law will have no power over
us.
164   *Steal forth :* creep out of.
165   *without :* outside.
167   To perform the rites of May Day.
168   *stay :* wait.

Hermia
O cross! too high to be enthrall'd to low.
Lysander
Or else misgraffed in respect of years—
Hermia
O spite! too old to be engag'd to young.
Lysander
Or else it stood upon the choice of friends—
Hermia
140 O hell! to choose love by another's eyes.
Lysander
Or, if there were a sympathy in choice,
War, death, or sickness did lay siege to it,
Making it momentary as a sound,
Swift as a shadow, short as any dream,
145 Brief as the lightning in the collied night,
That in a spleen unfolds both heaven and earth,
And ere a man hath power to say, 'Behold!'
The jaws of darkness do devour it up:
So quick bright things come to confusion.
Hermia
150 If then true lovers have been ever cross'd,
It stands as an edict in destiny.
Then let us teach our trial patience,
Because it is a customary cross,
As due to love as thoughts and dreams and sighs,
155 Wishes and tears, poor fancy's followers.
Lysander
A good persuasion. Therefore, hear me, Hermia:
I have a widow aunt, a dowager
Of great revenue, and she hath no child—
From Athens is her house remote seven leagues—
160 And she respects me as her only son.
There, gentle Hermia, may I marry thee,
And to that place the sharp Athenian law
Cannot pursue us. If thou lov'st me then,
Steal forth thy father's house tomorrow night,
165 And in the wood, a league without the town—
Where I did meet thee once with Helena,
To do observance to a morn of May—
There will I stay for thee.
Hermia   My good Lysander,

169   *Cupid :* the classical god of love, described by Helena in lines 234–41 of this scene (see p. vi, and illustration, p. 9).

170   *best . . . head :* Cupid had two arrows, one with a golden head to cause love and one with a leaden tip that killed all passion.

171   *Venus' doves :* The classical goddess of love was often pictured with white doves, which drew her chariot and brought messages. Their colour signified the innocence ('simplicity') of true love.

172   *that . . . loves :* perhaps Hermia is referring to the girdle worn by Venus.

173–4   When Dido, Queen of Carthage, saw her lover, the Trojan Aeneas, sailing away ('under sail') from her, she threw herself on a funeral pyre and was burned to death.

180   *God speed :* may God be with you.

182   *fair :* beauty.

183   *lodestars :* guiding stars; navigators at sea steer their courses by the pole star, and the Elizabethans also believed that this star had some magnetic power.
        air : sound.

184   *tuneable :* tuneful.

185   *hawthorn buds.* The hawthorn is one of the first trees to flower in the English springtime.

186   *catching :* infectious.
        favour : beauty, charm.

187   *ere :* before.

190   *bated :* excepted.

191   *translated :* transferred (to become Hermia's property).

193   *sway . . . heart :* influence the way Demetrius feels.

I swear to thee by Cupid's strongest bow,
170   By his best arrow with the golden head,
By the simplicity of Venus' doves,
By that which knitteth souls and prospers loves,
And by that fire which burn'd the Carthage queen
When the false Trojan under sail was seen;
175   By all the vows that ever men have broke—
In number more than ever women spoke—
In that same place thou hast appointed me
To-morrow truly will I meet with thee.

Lysander
Keep promise, love. Look, here comes Helena.

Enter Helena

Hermia
180   God speed, fair Helena! Whither away?

Helena
Call you me fair? That fair again unsay.
Demetrius loves your fair: O happy fair!
Your eyes are lodestars, and your tongue's sweet air
More tuneable than lark to shepherd's ear
185   When wheat is green, when hawthorn buds appear.
Sickness is catching: O were favour so,
Yours would I catch, fair Hermia, ere I go.
My ear should catch your voice, my eye your eye,
My tongue should catch your tongue's sweet melody.
190   Were the world mine, Demetrius being bated,
The rest I'd give to be to you translated.
O teach me how you look, and with what art
You sway the motion of Demetrius' heart.

Hermia
I frown upon him, yet he loves me still.

Helena
195   O that your frowns would teach my smiles such skill!

Hermia
I give him curses, yet he gives me love.

Helena
O that my prayers could such affection move!

Hermia
The more I hate, the more he follows me.

Helena

The more I love, the more he hateth me.

Hermia

200 His folly, Helena, is no fault of mine.

Helena

None but your beauty: would that fault were mine!

Hermia

Take comfort: he no more shall see my face;
Lysander and myself will fly this place.
Before the time I did Lysander see,
205 Seem'd Athens as a paradise to me:
O then, what graces in my love do dwell,
That he hath turn'd a heaven unto a hell.

Lysander

Helen, to you our minds we will unfold.
Tomorrow night, when Phœbe doth behold
210 Her silver visage in the wat'ry glass,
Decking with liquid pearl the bladed grass—
A time that lovers' flights doth still conceal—
Through Athens' gates have we devis'd to steal.

Hermia

And in the wood, where often you and I
215 Upon faint primrose-beds were wont to lie,
Emptying our bosoms of their counsel sweet,
There my Lysander and myself shall meet;
And thence from Athens turn away our eyes,
To seek new friends and stranger companies.
220 Farewell, sweet playfellow: pray thou for us;
And good luck grant thee thy Demetrius.
Keep word, Lysander: we must starve our sight
From lovers' food till morrow deep midnight.

Lysander

I will, my Hermia.   [*Exit* Hermia
                Helena, adieu:
225 As you on him, Demetrius dote on you.   [*Exit*

Helena

How happy some o'er other some can be!
Through Athens I am thought as fair as she;
But what of that? Demetrius thinks not so;
He will not know what all but he do know.
230 And as he errs, doting on Hermia's eyes,
So I, admiring of his qualities.

201 *would :* I wish.

203 *fly :* escape from.

206 *graces :* qualities.

208 *minds :* thoughts, plans.
      unfold : open, explain.
209 *Phoebe :* another name for the moon.
210 *visage :* face.
      wat'ry glass : mirror made by a stretch of water (a lake or pond).
211 *Decking :* trimming.
      liquid pearl : drops of dew (glistening like pearls); the Elizabethans thought that dew fell from the moon.
212 *still :* always.
213 *devis'd :* planned.
215 *faint :* delicate. The primrose is a pale yellow, slightly scented flower of early spring.
      wont : accustomed.
216 *bosoms :* hearts.
      counsel : secrets.
219 *stranger companies :* the company of people who are strangers to us.
222 *Keep word :* keep your promise.
223 *lovers' food :* i.e. the sight of each other.
      deep : dark.
225 May Demetrius love you as much as you love him.
226 How happy some people can be— much happier than others.
      o'er : over.
      other some : other people.

232 *holding no quantity* : having no value.

233 *transpose* : transform.

234 Love does not see the real, but the imaginary (what is in the mind).

235 *Cupid.* The god of love was depicted exactly as Helena describes— as a child, able to fly but not to see.

236 Love's mind is without reason (does not 'taste' of 'judgement').

237 *figure* : represent.
unheedy : thoughtless.

239 *beguil'd* : deceived.

240 *waggish* : playful.
in game : in fun.
themselves forswear : break promises.

241 Love, like a little boy, breaks his promises everywhere.

242 *ere* : until.
eyne : eyes.

248 *intelligence* : piece of information.

249 This line has more than one meaning: (i) for Demetrius, it will be an effort (and thus expensive) merely to give Helena thanks for the information, but (ii) a word of thanks from Demetrius will be precious ('dear') to Helena, even though (iii) she has paid a high price for it (in betraying her friend).

250 *herein* : in this way.
enrich my pain : reward myself for taking so much trouble.

251 By being with him (having sight of him) when he goes to the woods and when he returns.

Things base and vile, holding no quantity,
Love can transpose to form and dignity.
Love looks not with the eyes, but with the mind,
235 And therefore is wing'd Cupid painted blind.
Nor hath Love's mind of any judgement taste,
Wings and no eyes figure unheedy haste:
And therefore is Love said to be a child,
Because in choice he is so oft beguil'd.
240 As waggish boys in game themselves forswear,
So the boy Love is perjur'd everywhere;
For ere Demetrius look'd on Hermia's eyne,
He hail'd down oaths that he was only mine;
And when this hail some heat from Hermia felt,
245 So he dissolv'd, and show'rs of oaths did melt.
I will go tell him of fair Hermia's flight:
Then to the wood will he tomorrow night
Pursue her; and for this intelligence
If I have thanks, it is a dear expense:
250 But herein mean I to enrich my pain,
To have his sight thither and back again. [*Exit*

Act 1   Scene 2

Some Athenian workmen (their names indicate their trades—see p. vii) intend to produce a play in honour of their duke's marriage (p. iv). Peter Quince is the director, but Nick Bottom wants to act all the main parts himself.

2   *You were best :* you ought.
     generally. In his efforts to sound grand, Bottom sometimes uses words that do not mean what he intends: here he says 'generally' (=all together) when he means 'severally' (=separately).
3   *scrip :* list.
6   *interlude :* a short play (see Introduction, p. xvii).
8   *treats on :* is about.
10   *grow to a point :* reach a conclusion.
11   *Marry :* by the Virgin Mary (a mild oath).
15   *by the scroll :* according to the list.

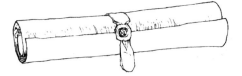

spread yourselves : sit down.

22   *let . . . eyes :* the audience must be careful not to weep too much.
23   *condole :* lament.
     in some measure : to a certain extent.
23–4 *To the rest :* now go on with the business.
24   *my chief . . . tyrant.* This has the double meaning of 'I would most of all like to play the part of a tyrant' and 'I am best suited to the part of a tyrant'.
25   *Ercles :* Hercules, the superman of Greek mythology.
25–6 *a part . . . split :* a part that demands violent action and language.

Scene 2   *Athens : Peter Quince's house*

Enter Quince, Snug, Bottom, Flute, Snout, *and* Starveling

Quince
Is all our company here?

Bottom
You were best to call them generally, man by man, according to the scrip.

Quince
Here is the scroll of every man's name, which is
5 thought fit, through all Athens, to play in our interlude before the duke and the duchess on his wedding-day at night.

Bottom
First, good Peter Quince, say what the play treats on; then read the names of the actors, and so grow to
10 a point.

Quince
Marry, our play is, *The most lamentable comedy, and most cruel death of Pyramus and Thisbe.*

Bottom
A very good piece of work, I assure you, and a merry. Now, good Peter Quince, call forth your
15 actors by the scroll. Masters, spread yourselves.

Quince
Answer as I call you. Nick Bottom, the weaver?

Bottom
Ready! Name what part I am for, and proceed.

Quince
You, Nick Bottom, are set down for Pyramus.

Bottom
What is Pyramus? A lover, or a tyrant?

Quince
20 A lover, that kills himself most gallant for love.

Bottom
That will ask some tears in the true performing of it : if I do it, let the audience look to their eyes! I will move storms; I will condole in some measure. To the rest—yet my chief humour is for a tyrant. I
25 could play Ercles rarely, or a part to tear a cat in, to make all split.

The raging rocks
And shivering shocks
Shall break the locks
    Of prison gates:
30
And Phibbus' car
Shall shine from far
And make and mar
    The foolish Fates.

35 This was lofty! Now name the rest of the players.
This is Ercles' vein, a tyrant's vein; a lover is more
condoling.
    Quince
Francis Flute, the bellows-mender?
    Flute
Here, Peter Quince.
    Quince
40 Flute, you must take Thisbe on you.
    Flute
What is Thisbe? A wandering knight?
    Quince
It is the lady that Pyramus must love.
    Flute
Nay, faith, let me not play a woman; I have a beard
coming.
    Quince
45 That's all one: you shall play it in a mask, and you
may speak as small as you will.
    Bottom
An I may hide my face, let me play Thisbe too. I'll
speak in a monstrous little voice: 'Thisne, Thisne!'
'Ah, Pyramus, my lover dear; thy Thisbe dear, and
50 lady dear!'
    Quince
No, no; you must play Pyramus; and Flute, you
Thisbe.
    Bottom
Well, proceed.
    Quince
Robin Starveling, the tailor.
    Starveling
55 Here, Peter Quince.
    Quince
Robin Starveling, you must play Thisbe's mother.

31   *Phibbus' car*: the chariot of the sun-god, Phoebus Apollo.

34   *Fates*: the three sisters who (in classical mythology) determined the course of every man's life.
36   *vein*: style.
37   *condoling*: pathetic.

38   *bellows*: an instrument used to blow air into organ-pipes or (domestically) on to coals to make the fire blaze.

43   *faith*: by my faith.
45   *That's all one*: that does not matter.
46   *small*: shrill (like a woman's voice).
47   *An*: if.
48–50 *Thisne . . . lady dear*. Bottom tries to make a diminutive form of 'Thisbe' to indicate Pyramus's affection. He speaks first as the lover, then replies as Thisbe.

Tom Snout, the tinker.

Snout

Here, Peter Quince.

Quince

60 You, Pyramus' father; myself, Thisbe's father;
Snug the joiner, you the lion's part: and, I hope,
here is a play fitted.

Snug

Have you the lion's part written? Pray you, if it be,
give it me, for I am slow of study.

Quince

You may do it extempore, for it is nothing but
65 roaring.

Bottom

Let me play the lion too. I will roar, that I will do
any man's heart good to hear me; I will roar, that I
will make the duke say, 'Let him roar again, let him
roar again'.

Quince

70 An you should do it too terribly, you would fright
the duchess and the ladies, that they would shriek;
and that were enough to hang us all.

All

That would hang us, every mother's son.

Bottom

I grant you, friends, if you should fright the
75 ladies out of their wits, they would have no more
discretion but to hang us; but I will aggravate my
voice so that I will roar you as gently as any sucking
dove; I will roar you an 'twere any nightingale.

Quince

You can play no part but Pyramus; for Pyramus is a
80 sweet-faced man; a proper man, as one shall see in a
summer's day; a most lovely, gentleman-like man;
therefore, you must needs play Pyramus.

Bottom

Well, I will undertake it. What beard were I best to
play it in?

Quince

85 Why, what you will.

Bottom

I will discharge it in either your straw-colour

---

59   *Pyramus . . . father :* neither of
these characters appears when the play
is finally performed.

61   *fitted :* cast.

63   *slow of study :* a slow learner.

64   *extempore :* without a script,
spontaneously.

66   *that :* so that.

70   *An :* if.
      fright : frighten.
71   *that :* so that.

Bottom – wants everything – full of himself – not any good

76   *aggravate :* make worse; Bottom
really wants a word like 'moderate'
(=control).
77   *roar you :* roar for you.
77–8   *sucking dove :* Bottom confuses
two models of gentleness—the sucking
lamb and the *sitting* dove.
78   *an 'twere :* as though it were.
      nightingale : a small bird that sings
very sweetly in the evening.
80   *sweet-faced :* handsome.
      proper : masculine.
82   *must needs :* must certainly.

86   *discharge :* perform.

87   *in-grain* : deeply dyed.
        French-crown-colour : light gold,
        the colour of a French coin.
90   Some French men have bald
        heads ('crowns'). Quince is making a
        joke, familiar to the Elizabethans,
        about the baldness caused by syphilis,
        which the English called 'the French
        disease'.
92   *I am to* : I must.
93   *con* : learn.
95   *without* : outside.

97   *dogged* : followed.
        devices : plans.
98   *bill* : list.
        properties : stage equipment.

101   *obscenely*. Bottom perhaps means
        'unseen', or 'seemly' (=properly).
        pains : care.
        be perfect : know your parts
        perfectly.
102   *adieu* : farewell (Bottom has
        learned a French word).
104   *hold . . . strings* : The meaning of
        this phrase is unknown, but Bottom
        appears to be saying that the actors
        must keep their promises ('hold'), or
        else be disgraced.

beard, your orange-tawny beard, your purple-in-grain beard, or your French-crown-colour beard, your perfect yellow.

Quince

90 Some of your French crowns have no hair at all, and then you will play bare-faced. But masters, here are your parts; and I am to entreat you, request you, and desire you, to con them by tomorrow night, and meet me in the palace wood, a mile without the

95 town, by moonlight. There will we rehearse; for if we meet in the city, we shall be dogged with company, and our devices known. In the meantime I will draw a bill of properties, such as our play wants. I pray you, fail me not.

Bottom

100 We will meet; and there we may rehearse most obscenely and courageously. Take pains; be perfect; adieu.

Quince

At the duke's oak we meet.

Bottom

Enough; hold, or cut bow-strings.   [*Exeunt*

Act 2

Act 2   Scene 1

A fairy, one of Titania's attendants,
describes the life and work of fairy
beings, and then identifies Puck and
relates some of the tricks that he plays
on mortals. The king and queen of the
fairies meet by accident; we hear about
their quarrelling, which is caused by
Titania's refusal to let her page-boy
become one of Oberon's followers.
Oberon plans his revenge, and sends
Puck to find a magic flower. Before
Oberon leaves the stage, however,
Demetrius enters, followed by Helena.
Oberon makes himself invisible to
them, and thus overhears the cruel
words that Demetrius addresses to the
love-sick Helena. When Puck returns
with the flower Oberon sends him to
use some of its magic to compel
Demetrius to love Helena.

2   *dale* : valley.
3   *Thorough* : an old form of
'through' (retained here for the sake of
the rhythm).
3   *brier* : thorn.

Scene 1   *A wood near Athens*

Enter a Fairy *on one side, and* Puck *on the
other*

Puck

How now, spirit! whither wander you?

Fairy

Over hill, over dale, *valley* *through*
   Thorough bush, thorough brier,
Over park, over pale, - *parks*
   Thorough flood, thorough fire,   5
I do wander everywhere,
Swifter than the moon's sphere;
And I serve the fairy queen,
To dew her orbs upon the green.
The cowslips tall her pensioners be;   10
In their gold coats spots you see:
Those be rubies, fairy favours,
In those freckles live their savours:

4   *pale* : piece of land enclosed by railings (palings); a 'park' was also enclosed—but the fairies have free access everywhere.

7   *moon's sphere* : circle of the moon.

9   *To dew* : to sprinkle with dew.

    her orbs : fairy rings—the name given to patches of unusually rich grass which were thought to be formed by the fairies' dancing (until modern scientists explained that in these areas the ground is unusually rich in nitrogen!).

10   *cowslips* : wild flowers with yellow, bell-shaped heads spotted with red. A tiny fairy would find these flowers (about 15 cm high) to be 'tall', but 'tall' also means 'handsome'—which would be appropriate to describe the royal bodyguard ('pensioners'), who would also be finely dressed (in 'gold coats' with jewels). See p. iv.

12   *favours* : gifts (indicating royal favour=approval).

16   *lob of spirits* : country oaf of the fairies (see p. ix).

17   *anon* : very soon.

19   *heed* : care.

20   *passing* : extremely.

    fell : fierce.

23   *changeling* : see Introduction, p. xiii.

24   *jealous* : envious.

25   *Knight of his train* : to be a knight in his service.

    trace : roam through.

26   *perforce* : forcibly.

29   *sheen* : shining.

30   *square* : quarrel.

    that : so that.

31   *acorn-cups* : the acorn (nut of an oak tree) grows on the branches in a cup-shaped holder (less than 2 cm diameter), from which it falls when ripe.

I must go seek some dew-drops here,
15 And hang a pearl in every cowslip's ear.
Farewell, thou lob of spirits : I'll be gone;
Our queen and all her elves come here anon.

Puck
The king doth keep his revels here to-night.
Take heed the queen come not within his sight;
20 For Oberon is passing fell and wrath,
Because that she as her attendant hath
A lovely boy, stol'n from an Indian king—
She never had so sweet a changeling—
And jealous Oberon would have the child
25 Knight of his train, to trace the forests wild.
But she perforce withholds the loved boy,
Crowns him with flowers, and makes him all her joy.
And now they never meet in grove, or green,
By fountain clear, or spangled starlight sheen,
30 But they do square, that all their elves for fear
Creep into acorn-cups and hide them there.

COWSLIP

32   *making :* appearance.

32   *quite :* completely.

33   *shrewd :* crafty.
    knavish : mischievous.
    sprite : spirit.

34   *Robin Goodfellow :* see p. x.

35   *villagery :* village people.

36   *Skim milk :* take the cream from
the milk. (*Note:* Shakespeare has
forgotten that his last subject was the
pronoun 'he' and that the verb form
should be 3rd person singular [as at
line 35 'frights']; the fairy, speaking
directly to Puck, has returned to the
use of the 2nd person singular [as at
line 33 'you are']. Although we try to
avoid such confusion today, it would
not have worried Shakespeare's
contemporaries.)
    quern : churn—the container in
which milk is violently stirred
(churned) to turn the cream into
butter. Puck's activities (when he
labours) inside the churn make the
housewife struggle without result
('bootless').

38   *barm :* froth (which should always
be present on top of good home-
brewed ale).

39   In *Act 3* scene 2 we can see how
Puck does this.

44   *jest :* joke (Puck claims to be
Oberon's professional jester).

46   *filly :* female.

47   *gossip :* old woman.

48   *very :* true.
    crab : crab apple—a kind of very
small apple that was often roasted and
added, as a spice, to ale.

50   *dewlap :* the folds of skin hanging
round an old person's throat.

51   *aunt :* old woman.

52   *three-foot stool :* a small, probably
round, seat with three legs.

Fairy
Either I mistake your shape and making quite,
Or else you are that shrewd and knavish sprite
Call'd Robin Goodfellow: are not you he

35 That frights the maidens of the villagery;
Skim milk, and sometimes labour in the quern,
And bootless make the breathless housewife churn;
And sometime make the drink to bear no barm;
Mislead night-wanderers, laughing at their harm?

40 Those that 'Hobgoblin' call you, and 'Sweet Puck',
You do their work, and they shall have good luck.
Are not you he?
    Puck   Thou speak'st aright;
I am that merry wanderer of the night.
I jest to Oberon, and make him smile

45 When I a fat and bean-fed horse beguile,
Neighing in likeness of a filly foal;
And sometime lurk I in a gossip's bowl,
In very likeness of a roasted crab,
And when she drinks, against her lips I bob,

50 And on her wither'd dewlap pour the ale.
The wisest aunt, telling the saddest tale,
Sometime for three-foot stool mistaketh me;

CHURNING BUTTER

Hey, Do it Harder

54   *Tailor* : cheat.
      falls into a cough : starts coughing.
55   *quire* : company.
56   *waxen* : increase.
      neeze : sneeze.
57   *wasted* : spent.
58   *room* : make room.
59   *Would* : I wish.
60   *Ill met* : an unlucky meeting.
61   *jealous* : envious.
62   *forsworn* : refused.
      Tarry : Wait!
63   *rash wanton* : headstrong, wilful
      creature.
      lord : husband (and therefore
      entitled to respect from his wife).
64   *lady* : wife (and therefore entitled
      to expect faithfulness from her
      husband).
66   *shape* : appearance.
      Corin : the name traditionally
      given (in classical literature) to love-
      sick shepherds; *Phillida* (line 68) was
      the feminine equivalent.
67   *pipes of corn* : musical pipes made
      out of corn stalks.
67   *versing love* : singing love songs.
69   *steep* : hill (perhaps the Himalayan
      Mountains).
70   *But* : except.
      forsooth : indeed.
      bouncing : physically energetic.
      Amazon : see p. vi.

Then slip I from her bum, down topples she,
And 'Tailor' cries, and falls into a cough;
55 And then the whole quire hold their hips and
    laugh,
And waxen in their mirth, and neeze, and swear
A merrier hour was never wasted there.
But room, fairy! Here comes Oberon.
         Fairy
And here my mistress. Would that he were gone!

         Enter Oberon *from one side, with his
         Attendants; and* Titania *from the other,
         with hers*

    Oberon
60 Ill met by moonlight, proud Titania.
    Titania
What, jealous Oberon! Fairies, skip hence:
I have forsworn his bed and company.
    Oberon
Tarry, rash wanton! Am not I thy lord?
    Titania
Then I must be thy lady. But I know
65 When thou hast stol'n away from Fairyland,
And in the shape of Corin sat all day,
Playing on pipes of corn, and versing love
To amorous Phillida. Why art thou here,
Come from the farthest steep of India,
70 But that, forsooth, the bouncing Amazon,

AN AMAZON

71 *buskin'd :* wearing high boots.
       warrior : see p. vi.
73 *give their bed :* bless their union
       with.
75 *Glance at :* make rude remarks
       about.
       credit : success (in winning the
       affection).
77–80 See p. viii.
81 *forgeries :* falsehoods.
82 *middle summer's spring :* beginning
       of the midsummer period.
83 *dale :* valley.
       mead : meadow.
84 *paved fountain :* fountain with
       small pebbles at the bottom.
       rushy brook : small stream with tall
       rushes growing at the sides.
85 *beached margent :* beach at the edge
       (margin).
86 *ringlets :* dances round the fairy
       rings (see line 9).
       whistling wind : the wind whistled
       as music for their dancing.
87 *brawls :* quarrels.
       sport : entertainment.
88 *in vain :* uselessly.
89 *As in revenge :* as though they
       were taking revenge.
90 *Contagious :* carrying diseases,
       infectious.
91 *pelting :* paltry.
92 *overborne their continents :* flooded
       over their banks.
93 See illustration p. 4.
94 *lost his sweat :* wasted his effort
       (which made him sweat).
       green : unripe; ripe corn has
       hanging tendrils, like a man's beard.
95 *ere :* before.
96 *fatted :* grown fat.
       murrion flock : sheep and cattle
       killed by the disease called 'murraine'.
97–100 Nine-men's-morris was a popular
       summer game, played on ground
       especially cut out into elaborate paths
       ('quaint mazes'). Now mud has filled
       up the pathways, no-one treads in
       them, and they cannot be identified
       through the grass ('green') that has
       become overgrown ('wanton').

Your buskin'd mistress and your warrior love,
To Theseus must be wedded, and you come
To give their bed joy and prosperity.

Oberon

How canst thou thus, for shame, Titania,
75 Glance at my credit with Hippolyta,
Knowing I know thy love to Theseus?
Didst not thou lead him through the glimmering
      night
From Perigouna, whom he ravished?
And make him with fair Aegles break his faith,
80 With Ariadne, and Antiopa?

Titania

These are the forgeries of jealousy:
And never, since the middle summer's spring,
Met we on hill, in dale, forest, or mead,
By paved fountain, or by rushy brook,
85 Or in the beached margent of the sea,
To dance our ringlets to the whistling wind,
But with thy brawls thou hast disturb'd our sport.
Therefore the winds, piping to us in vain,
As in revenge, have suck'd up from the sea
90 Contagious fogs which, falling in the land,
Hath every pelting river made so proud
That they have overborne their continents:
The ox hath therefore stretch'd his yoke in vain,
The ploughman lost his sweat, and the green corn
95 Hath rotted ere his youth attain'd a beard:
The fold stands empty in the drowned field,
And crows are fatted with the murrion flock;
The nine-men's-morris is fill'd up with mud,
And the quaint mazes in the wanton green
100 For lack of tread are undistinguishable.

NINE-MEN'S MORRIS

101 *want :* are deprived of.
     cheer : festivities.
103 *governess of floods :* the
     relationship between the moon and the
     earth is partly responsible for
     (governs) the tidal movements of the
     sea.
104 *washes :* there was a belief that the
     moon shed moisture on the earth.
105 *rheumatic diseases :* not only the
     modern 'rheumatism' but also colds
     and influenza, where a rheum (=a
     watery discharge) comes from eyes and
     nose. (The word is stressed
     'rheumatic' here.)
     do abound : are very common.
106 *thorough :* through.
     distemperature : disturbance in the
     weather (temperature).
107 *hoary-headed frosts :* anything
     affected by frost is white ('hoary') on
     the surface.
109 *Hiems :* a common personification
     of winter as an old man with little hair
     on his head ('crown'); the name is the
     Latin word for winter.
110 *odorous :* scented.
     chaplet : wreath worn on the head.
111 *as in mockery :* as though making
     fun of the old man.
112 *childing :* fruitful (bearing
     children).
113 *wonted liveries :* usual clothing.
     mazed : bewildered.
114 Cannot distinguish, by what they
     produce ('their increase') one season
     from another. (Winter should be
     recognized by its frosts, and summer
     by its flowers.)
115 *progeny :* offspring.
116 *debate :* arguing.
117 *original :* origin.
     Do you : you can.
118 *amend :* improve.
     it lies in you : it is in your power.
119 *cross :* disobey.
120 *but :* only.
121 *henchman :* page.
     Set . . . rest : be assured.
122 *of :* from.

The human mortals want their winter cheer:
No night is now with hymn or carol blest.
Therefore the moon, the governess of floods,
Pale in her anger, washes all the air,
105 That rheumatic diseases do abound:
And thorough this distemperature we see
The seasons alter: hoary-headed frosts
Fall in the fresh lap of the crimson rose,
And on old Hiems' thin and icy crown
110 An odorous chaplet of sweet summer buds
Is, as in mockery, set. The spring, the summer,
The childing autumn, angry winter, change
Their wonted liveries, and the mazed world,
By their increase, now knows not which is which.
115 And this same progeny of evils comes
From our debate, from our dissension:
We are their parents and original.
     Oberon
Do you amend it then: it lies in you.
Why should Titania cross her Oberon?
120 I do but beg a little changeling boy,
To be my henchman,
     Titania   Set your heart at rest;
The fairy land buys not the child of me.

fighting over
little indian page boy

[Handwritten annotation at top: India Boy is mortal—mortual friend of Titania]

123   *votress :* woman who has taken religious vows (such as a nun).
    of my order : of the religion which held Titania in respect.
124   *spiced :* fragrant.
126   *Neptune :* god of the sea (in classical mythology).
127   *Marking :* observing.
    embarked traders : trading ships.
    on the flood : as the tide brought them to shore (flood-tide is the incoming tide).
128   *conceive :* swell (as though pregnant).

129   *wanton :* playful, amorous.
130   *swimming :* gliding.
    gait : movement.
131   *Following :* copying.
    rich : pregnant.
    squire : gentleman (especially one who attends a lady).
135   *of that boy :* giving birth to the boy.
138   *intend you stay :* do you intend to stay?
139   *Perchance :* perhaps.
140   *patiently :* without complaining.
    round : circular dance.
142   *spare :* avoid.
    haunts : favourite places.
145   *chide :* quarrel.
    downright : absolutely.

His mother was a votress of my order:
And in the spiced Indian air, by night,
125 Full often hath she gossip'd by my side,
And sat with me on Neptune's yellow sands,
Marking th' embarked traders on the flood,
When we have laugh'd to see the sails conceive
And grow big-bellied with the wanton wind;
130 Which she, with pretty and with swimming gait
Following—her womb then rich with my young squire—
Would imitate, and sail upon the land
To fetch me trifles, and return again,
As from a voyage, rich with merchandise.
135 But she, being mortal, of that boy did die;
And for her sake do I rear up her boy,
And for her sake I will not part with him.

Oberon

How long within this wood intend you stay?

Titania

Perchance till after Theseus' wedding-day.
140 If you will patiently dance in our round,
And see our moonlight revels, go with us;
If not, shun me, and I will spare your haunts.

Oberon

Give me that boy, and I will go with thee.

Titania

Not for thy fairy kingdom. Fairies, away!
145 We shall chide downright, if I longer stay.

[*Exit* Titania *with her Attendants*

146 *not from*: not go from.
147 *injury*: insult.
149 *Since once*: the time when.
    promontory: piece of land jutting
    out into the sea.
150 *mermaid*: a mythical creature,
    half-woman and half-fish, whose
    singing was enchanting.
        dolphin: a sea-dwelling mammal,
    friendly to humans and believed (even
    today) to be unusually intelligent.
151 *dulcet*: sweet-sounding.
    breath: song.
152 *rude*: rough (badly behaved).
    civil: calm (well behaved).
153 *spheres*: orbits.
155 *very*: same.
156 *cold*: without heat; also 'chaste',
    because Diana, the goddess of the
    moon, was also goddess of chastity.
157 See p. xxii.
158 *vestal*: virgin; the Roman Vestal
    Virgins vowed eternal virginity, in
    service to Vesta, goddess of the home.
159 *love-shaft*: arrow of love.
160 *As it*: as though it.
161 *might*: was able to.
    fiery: i.e. because it produced the
    fires of love.
162 The moon was able to take away
    the power of Cupid's arrow because
    the moon is associated with both water
    and chastity (see notes to lines 104 and
    155).
163 *imperial*: royal.
    votress: female member of
    religious order.
164 *maiden*: virgin.
    fancy-free: with no thought of
    love.
165 *mark'd*: observed.
    bolt: arrow.

Oberon
Well, go thy way: thou shalt not from this grove
Till I torment thee for this injury.
My gentle Puck, come hither. Thou rememb'rest
Since once I sat upon a promontory,
150 And heard a mermaid on a dolphin's back
Uttering such dulcet and harmonious breath
That the rude sea grew civil at her song,
And certain stars shot madly from their spheres
To hear the sea-maid's music.
Puck   I remember.

Oberon
155 That very time I saw—but thou couldst not—
Flying between the cold moon and the earth,
Cupid all arm'd: a certain aim he took
At a fair vestal throned by the west,
And loos'd his love-shaft smartly from his bow,
160 As it should pierce a hundred thousand hearts;
But I might see young Cupid's fiery shaft
Quench'd in the chaste beams of the wat'ry moon,
And the imperial votress pass'd on,
In maiden meditation, fancy-free.
165 Yet mark'd I where the bolt of Cupid fell:

166   *western flower* : i.e. the pansy,
which is usually purple (or white, or
white streaked with purple).

168   *love-in-idleness* : love is associated
with idleness because busy people
have no time for love.
171   *or . . . or* : either . . . or.
174   *Ere* : before.
leviathan : whale.
league : measurement of distance
(about three miles).
175   *put a girdle* : encircle.
181   *busy* : mischievous.
183   *ere* : before.
186   *I am invisible.* With this statement
Oberon explains to the audience that
the human characters on stage are
unable to see him; in performance, he
might throw a dark cloak round
himself.
187   *conference* : conversation.
190   *slayeth me* : Demetrius asserts that
Hermia is killing him because she
refuses to love him.
191   *stol'n* : escaped from.
192   *and wood* : and mad.
195   *adamant* : Helena intends both
meanings of this word: 'magnet' and
'very hard stone'.
196–7   Although she is drawn towards
Demetrius as iron is drawn to a
magnet, Helena's heart is not made of
iron (which is merely hard) but has the
trusted faithfulness of steel ('true as
steel' is a proverbial expression).

It fell upon a little western flower,
Before milk-white, now purple with love's wound,
And maidens call it 'love-in-idleness'.
Fetch me that flower—the herb I show'd thee once.
170   The juice of it on sleeping eyelids laid
Will make or man or woman madly dote
Upon the next live creature that it sees.
Fetch me this herb; and be thou here again
Ere the leviathan can swim a league.

Puck

175   I'll put a girdle round about the earth
In forty minutes.   [*Exit*

Oberon   Having once this juice
I'll watch Titania when she is asleep,
And drop the liquor of it in her eyes:
The next thing then she waking looks upon—
180   Be it on lion, bear, or wolf, or bull,
On meddling monkey, or on busy ape—
She shall pursue it with the soul of love.
And ere I take this charm from off her sight,
(As I can take it with another herb)
185   I'll make her render up her page to me.
But who comes here? I am invisible,
And I will overhear their conference.

Enter Demetrius, Helena *following him*

Demetrius

I love thee not, therefore pursue me not.
Where is Lysander and fair Hermia?
190   The one I'll slay, the other slayeth me.
Thou told'st me they were stol'n unto this wood;
And here am I, and wood within this wood,
Because I cannot meet my Hermia.
Hence, get thee gone, and follow me no more!

Helena

195   You draw me, you hard-hearted adamant:
But yet you draw not iron, for my heart
Is true as steel; leave you your power to draw,
And I shall have no power to follow you.

197   *leave you :* if you will give up.
199   *speak you fair :* say kind words to
you.

203   *spaniel :* dog used in hunting to
retrieve game from water; spaniels
have a reputation for faithfulness even
when they are badly treated.

204   *fawn :* cringe, beg for favour.
205   *spurn :* kick.
214   *impeach your modesty :* cause your
modesty to be suspected.
217–9   To trust that your precious
virginity will be safe when the night
gives an opportunity, and the lonely
place offers temptation.
220   *virtue :* particular nature.
privilege : protection.
for that : because.
224   *respect :* opinion.
227   *brakes :* bushes.

Demetrius
Do I entice you? Do I speak you fair?
200 Or, rather, do I not in plainest truth
Tell you I do not nor I cannot love you?
Helena
And even for that do I love you the more.
I am your spaniel; and, Demetrius,
The more you beat me, I will fawn on you:
205 Use me but as your spaniel, spurn me, strike me,
Neglect me, lose me; only give me leave,
Unworthy as I am, to follow you.
What worser place can I beg in your love—
And yet a place of high respect with me—
210 Than to be used as you use your dog?
Demetrius
Tempt not too much the hatred of my spirit,
For I am sick when I do look on thee.
Helena
And I am sick when I look not on you.
Demetrius
You do impeach your modesty too much,
215 To leave the city, and commit yourself
Into the hands of one that loves you not;
To trust the opportunity of night
And the ill counsel of a desert place
With the rich worth of your virginity.
Helena
220 Your virtue is my privilege: for that
It is not night when I do see your face,
Therefore I think I am not in the night;
Nor doth this wood lack worlds of company,
For you in my respect are all the world;
225 Then how can it be said I am alone,
When all the world is here to look on me?
Demetrius
I'll run from thee and hide me in the brakes,
And leave thee to the mercy of wild beasts.
Helena
The wildest hath not such a heart as you.
230 Run when you will. The story shall be chang'd:

231   In classical mythology, Apollo fell
in love with Daphne and ran after her
(she prayed to Diana for protection
and was changed into a laurel tree).

232   *griffin :* a fabulous monster, with
head and wings of an eagle and the
body of a man.
       hind : female deer.

233   *bootless :* useless.

235   *stay your questions :* wait to hear
your arguments.

237   *But :* but that.

238   *do thee mischief :* harm you.

240   *wrongs :* ill-treatment.
       set . . . sex : make me act in a way
that is improper for a woman.

245   *nymph :* girl.

246   *fly him :* run away from him.

249   *wild thyme :* a low-growing
scented herb with tiny purple flowers.
       blows : blossoms.

250   *oxlips :* flower slightly bigger than
the cowslip.

251   *woodbine :* honey-suckle, a
climbing plant that makes a shelter
(canopy) over the bank.

252   *musk-roses :* these also climb, and
are heavily scented.
       eglantine : another kind of wild
rose.

253   *some time :* for some period.

254   *Lull'd :* sent to sleep.

255   *throws :* sheds (snakes regularly
shed their skins when a new one has
grown beneath the old).
       enamell'd : smooth and coloured.

256   *Weed wide enough :* a garment that
is wide enough.

Apollo flies, and Daphne holds the chase;
The dove pursues the griffin; the mild hind
Makes speed to catch the tiger—bootless speed,
When cowardice pursues and valour flies.

Demetrius

235 I will not stay thy questions. Let me go;
Or, if thou follow me, do not believe
But I shall do thee mischief in the wood.

Helena

Ay, in the temple, in the town, the field,
You do me mischief. Fie, Demetrius!

240 Your wrongs do set a scandal on my sex.
We cannot fight for love, as men may do;
We should be woo'd and were not made to woo.
                              [*Exit* Demetrius
I'll follow thee and make a heaven of hell,
To die upon the hand I love so well.   [*Exit*

Oberon

Fare thee well, nymph. Ere he do leave this grove,
246 Thou shalt fly him, and he shall seek thy love.

Enter Puck

Hast thou the flower there? Welcome, wanderer.

Puck

Ay, there it is.

Oberon   I pray thee, give it me.
I know a bank where the wild thyme blows,
250 Where oxlips and the nodding violet grows,
Quite over-canopied with luscious woodbine,
With sweet musk-roses, and with eglantine:
There sleeps Titania some time of the night,
Lull'd in these flowers with dances and delight.
255 And there the snake throws her enamell'd skin,
Weed wide enough to wrap a fairy in.

257   *streak : smear.*
262   *espies : looks on.*
265   *Effect : perform.*
267   *look thou : see that you.*
      cock crow : the cock crows at
dawn, when all supernatural beings
must leave the world of men.
However, Oberon says later in the play
that he and the other fairies are not
confined to the hours of darkness
(*3, 2, 388*).

And with the juice of this I'll streak her eyes,
And make her full of hateful fantasies.
Take thou some of it, and seek through this grove:
260 A sweet Athenian lady is in love
With a disdainful youth: anoint his eyes;
But do it when the next thing he espies
May be the lady. Thou shalt know the man
By the Athenian garments he hath on.
265 Effect it with some care, that he may prove
More fond on her than she upon her love.
And look thou meet me ere the first cock crow.

Puck
Fear not, my lord, your servant shall do so.

[*Exeunt*

Act 2   Scene 2
Titania gives instuctions to her fairy
attendants, then sends them away to
work. They leave her sleeping, and
Oberon takes the opportunity to put
the love-juice on her eyes. Hermia and
Lysander arrive in this part of the
wood; they are tired, and lie down to
sleep. Puck comes in search of
Demetrius, and assumes that Lysander
is the man he is looking for. He
sprinkles the love-juice (intended for
Demetrius) on Lysander's eyes.
Lysander wakes—and falls in love with
Helena.

1   *roundel :* dance in a circle.
3   *cankers :* small worms.
4   *war :* fight.
      reremice : bats.
7   *quaint :* dainty.
8   *to your offices :* go and do your duties.
9   *double :* forked.
10   *thorny :* with spikes.
11   *blind-worms :* slow-worms; the
Elizabethans wrongly believed that
these, and newts, were poisonous.
13   *Philomel :* classical name for the
nightingale.
14   *nigh :* near to.

Scene 2 *Another part of the wood*

Enter Titania, *with her Attendants*

Titania
Come, now a roundel and a fairy song,
Then, for the third part of a minute, hence:
Some to kill cankers in the musk-rose buds,
Some war with reremice for their leathern wings
5 To make my small elves coats, and some keep back
The clamorous owl, that nightly hoots, and
      wonders
At our quaint spirits. Sing me now asleep;
Then to your offices, and let me rest.

The Fairies sing

You spotted snakes with double tongue,
      Thorny hedgehogs, be not seen;
10 Newts and blind-worms, do no wrong,
      Come not near our fairy queen.

Philomel, with melody,
      Sing in our sweet lullaby;
15 Lulla, lulla, lullaby; lulla, lulla, lullaby.
      Never harm,

Nor spell, nor charm,
Come our lovely lady nigh;
So good night, with lullaby.

20   *spiders* : these were also thought to
be poisonous.

20   Weaving spiders come not here;
    Hence, you long-legg'd spinners, hence!
Beetles black, approach not near;
    Worm nor snail, do no offence.

25   Philomel, with melody,
    Sing in our sweet lullaby;
Lulla, lulla, lullaby; lulla, lulla, lullaby.
    Never harm,
    Nor spell, nor charm,
    Come our lovely lady nigh;
30   So good night with lullaby.

Fairy
Hence, away! Now all is well.
One aloof stand sentinel.

32   *stand sentinel* : keep guard.

[*Exeunt Fairies.* Titania *sleeps*

Enter Oberon, *and squeezes the flower on*
Titania's *eyelids*

Oberon
What thou seest when thou dost wake,
Do it for thy true-love take;
35   Love and languish for his sake.
Be it ounce, or cat, or bear,
Pard, or boar with bristled hair,
In thy eye that shall appear
When thou wak'st, it is thy dear.
40   Wake when some vile thing is near. [*Exit*

36   *ounce* : lynx.
37   *Pard* : leopard.

Enter Lysander *and* Hermia

Lysander
Fair love, you faint with wandering in the wood;
And to speak truth, I have forgot our way.
We'll rest us, Hermia, if you think it good,
And tarry for the comfort of the day.

44   *tarry* : wait.

Hermia
45   Be it so, Lysander: find you out a bed,
For I upon this bank will rest my head.

*Whatever Lysander — find yourself
a bed — I'm sleeping here*

Lysander
One turf shall serve as pillow for us both;
One heart, one bed, two bosoms, and one troth.

48   *troth* : faith.

Hermia
Nay, good Lysander; for my sake, my dear,
50 Lie further off yet, do not lie so near.

50   *further off yet* : still further away from.

Lysander
O, take the sense, sweet, of my innocence:
Love takes the meaning in love's conference.
I mean that my heart unto yours is knit,
So that but one heart we can make of it;
55 Two bosoms interchained with an oath—
So then two bosoms and a single troth.
Then by your side no bed-room me deny,
For lying so, Hermia, I do not lie.

51   Understand the real meaning ('sense') of my innocent remark.
52   Love interprets what is said in the conversation ('conference') between lovers.
53   *knit* : inextricably joined together.
54   *but one* : only one.
55   *interchained* : linked.
56   *troth* : bond of love.

Hermia
Lysander riddles very prettily.
60 Now much beshrew my manners and my pride,
If Hermia meant to say Lysander lied.
But, gentle friend, for love and courtesy,
Lie further off, in human modesty:
Such separation as may well be said
65 Becomes a virtuous bachelor and a maid,
So far be distant; and, good night, sweet friend.
Thy love ne'er alter till thy sweet life end!

58   Although Lysander wishes to sleep next to Hermia ('lying so'), he does not want to deceive ('lie' to) her.
59   *riddles* : plays with words.
     prettily : cleverly.
60   *much beshrew* : I really curse (Hermia is only half-serious).
61   *lied* : told a lie.
62   *for* : for the sake of.
66   *So far be distant* : keep just so far away.

Lysander
Amen, amen, to that fair prayer say I;
And then end life when I end loyalty!
            [*Moves away a little distance*
70 Here is my bed: sleep give thee all his rest.

Hermia
With half that wish the wisher's eyes be press'd.
                        [*They sleep*

Enter Puck

Puck
Through the forest have I gone,
But Athenian found I none
On whose eyes I might approve
75 This flower's force in stirring love.
Night and silence! who is here?
Weeds of Athens he doth wear:
This is he my master said

74   *approve* : test.
75   *force . . . love* : power to awaken love.
77   *Weeds* : garments.
78   *he my master said* : the man that my master said.

Despised the Athenian maid;
80 And here the maiden, sleeping sound
On the dank and dirty ground.
Pretty soul! she durst not lie
Near this lack-love, this kill-courtesy.
　　　　　[*Squeezes the flower on* Lysander's *eyelids*]
Churl, upon thy eyes I throw
85 All the power this charm doth owe.
When thou wak'st, let love forbid
Sleep his seat on thy eyelid:
So awake when I am gone,
For I must now to Oberon.　　　　　[*Exit*

　　　　　Enter Demetrius *and* Helena, *running*

Helena
90 Stay, though thou kill me, sweet Demetrius!
Demetrius
I charge thee hence, and do not haunt me thus.
Helena
O wilt thou darkling leave me? Do not so.
Demetrius
Stay, on thy peril: I alone will go. [*Exit* Demetrius
Helena
O, I am out of breath in this fond chase.
95 The more my prayer, the lesser is my grace.
Happy is Hermia, wheresoe'er she lies;
For she hath blessed and attractive eyes.
How came her eyes so bright? Not with salt tears:
If so, my eyes are oftener wash'd than hers.
100 No, no, I am as ugly as a bear;
For beasts that meet me run away for fear.
Therefore no marvel though Demetrius
Do as a monster fly my presence thus.
What wicked and dissembling glass of mine
105 Made me compare with Hermia's sphery eyne?
But who is here? Lysander! on the ground!
Dead? or asleep? I see no blood, no wound.
Lysander, if you live, good sir, awake.
Lysander　　　　　[*Waking*]
And run through fire I will for thy sweet sake.
110 Transparent Helena! Nature shows art
That through thy bosom makes me see thy heart.

82　　*durst*: dares.
83　　*lack-love*: man who does not love her.
　　　kill-courtesy: one whose rudeness destroys courtesy.
84　　*Churl*: brute.
85　　*owe*: possess.
86–7　*let . . . eyelid*: may love make you sleepless (by refusing to allow sleep to settle on his eyes).

91　　*charge you hence*: command you to go away.
　　　haunt: pursue.
92　　*darkling*: in the dark.

94　　*fond*: foolish.
95　　*the . . . grace*: the less favour do I receive.

103　 *as a monster*: as though I were a monster.
104　 *glass*: mirror.
105　 *sphery*: like stars.
　　　eyne: eyes.

110　 *Transparent*: glorious; Lysander proceeds to play on the more usual meaning (= able to be seen through).
　　　art: magic.

Where is Demetrius? O how fit a word
Is that vile name to perish on my sword.
Helena
Do not say so, Lysander, say not so.

115 What though he love your Hermia? Lord what
    though?
Yet Hermia still loves you: then be content.
Lysander
Content with Hermia! No, I do repent
The tedious minutes I with her have spent.
Not Hermia but Helena I love:
120 Who will not change a raven for a dove?
The will of man is by his reason sway'd,
And reason says you are the worthier maid.
Things growing are not ripe until their season:
So I, being young, till now ripe not to reason;
125 And touching now the point of human skill,
Reason becomes the marshal to my will,
And leads me to your eyes; where I o'erlook
Love's stories written in love's richest book.
Helena
Wherefore was I to this keen mockery born?
130 When at your hands did I deserve this scorn?
Is't not enough, is't not enough, young man,
That I did never, no, nor never can,
Deserve a sweet look from Demetrius' eye,
But you must flout my insufficiency?
135 Good troth, you do me wrong—good sooth, you
    do—
In such disdainful manner me to woo.
But fare you well. Perforce I must confess
I thought you lord of more true gentleness.
O that a lady of one man refus'd,
140 Should of another therefore be abus'd.   [*Exit*
Lysander
She sees not Hermia. Hermia, sleep thou there;
And never mayst thou come Lysander near.
For, as a surfeit of the sweetest things
The deepest loathing to the stomach brings;
145 Or as the heresies that men do leave
Are hated most of those they did deceive:
So thou, my surfeit and my heresy,
Of all be hated, but the most of me!

115   *what though*: what does it matter?

121   *will*: desire.

124   *till . . . reason*: was not mature in judgement until now.
125   And now reaching the top of human discrimination.
126   *marshal*: director.
      will: desire.
127   *o'erlook*: read over.
129   *Wherefore*: why?
      keen: cruel.

134   *insufficiency*: unattractiveness.
135   *Good troth*: indeed.
      good sooth: really.

137   *Perforce*: indeed.
138   *gentleness*: courtesy.
139   *of*: by.

143   *surfeit of*: over-indulgence in.
145–6   Discarded heresies (=false beliefs) are hated most by those people who once believed in them.
148   *of me*: by me.

Get this snake off me!
What a dream!

And, all my powers, address your love and might
150 To honour Helen, and to be her knight.   [*Exit*

Hermia *Help*   [*Waking*]
Help me, Lysander, help me! Do thy best
To pluck this crawling serpent from my breast!
Ay me, for pity! What a dream was here!
Lysander, look how I do quake with fear!
155 Methought a serpent ate my heart away,
And you sat smiling at his cruel prey.
Lysander! what, remov'd?—Lysander! lord!
What, out of hearing? Gone? No sound, no word?
Alack, where are you? Speak an if you hear;
160 Speak, of all loves! I swoon almost with fear.
No? Then I well perceive you are not nigh:
Either death or you I'll find immediately.
                                               [*Exit*

153   *Ay me, for pity :* oh dear, for pity's sake.

156   *prey :* act of preying on something.
157   *remov'd :* gone away.

159   *an if :* if.
160   *of all loves :* by all true loves.
161   *nigh :* near.

dreamt a snake was eating out her heart –
Lysander is gone when she awakes

Lysander → Helena → Demetrius → Hermia

Act 3

Woodsman—practicing play

Act 3 Scene 1

The Athenian workmen have met in the forest to rehearse their play. They discuss the problems of staging 'Pyramus and Thisbe', and then proceed to the acting. Puck discovers them, and seizes the chance to put a donkey's head on Bottom. This frightens the other workmen, who run away; but Titania (under the influence of Oberon's love-juice) immediately falls in love with Bottom and commands her fairies to serve him as their master.

2   *Pat, pat :* most punctually.

4   *hawthorn-brake :* bush of hawthorn (a thick shrub, with small white flowers).

    tiring-house : green-room (the area behind the stage where actors wait to hear their cues).

5   *in action :* with gestures and movement (not merely reading the script).

7   *bully :* good fellow.

11   *abide :* endure.

12   *By'r lakin :* by Our Lady.
    parlous : terrible.

Scene 1 *The wood ; Titania lies asleep*

Enter Quince, Snug, Bottom, Flute, Snout, *and* Starveling.

Bottom
Are we all met?

Quince
Pat, pat; and here's a marvellous convenient place for our rehearsal. This green plot shall be our stage, this hawthorn-brake our tiring-house; and we will
5 do it in action as we will do it before the duke.

Bottom
Peter Quince!

Quince
What sayest thou, bully Bottom?

Bottom
There are things in this comedy of Pyramus and Thisbe that will never please. First, Pyramus must
10 draw a sword to kill himself, which the ladies cannot abide. How answer you that?

Snout
By'r lakin, a parlous fear!

Starveling

I believe we must leave the killing out, when all is done.

Bottom

15   Not a whit: I have a device to make all well. Write me a prologue, and let the prologue seem to say we will do no harm with our swords, and that Pyramus is not killed indeed; and, for the more better assurance, tell them that I, Pyramus, am not
20   Pyramus, but Bottom the weaver. This will put them out of fear.

Quince

Well, we will have such a prologue; and it shall be written in eight and six.

Bottom

No, make it two more: let it be written in eight and
25   eight.

Snout

Will not the ladies be afeard of the lion?

Starveling

I fear it, I promise you.

Bottom

Masters, you ought to consider with yourselves. To bring in—God shield us!—a lion among ladies, is a
30   most dreadful thing; for there is not a more fearful wildfowl than your lion living, and we ought to look to it.

Snout

Therefore, another prologue must tell he is not a lion.

Bottom

35   Nay, you must name his name, and half his face must be seen through the lion's neck, and he himself must speak through, saying thus, or to the same defect, 'Ladies', or, 'Fair ladies—I would wish you', or, 'I would request you', or, 'I would
40   entreat you—not to fear, not to tremble. My life for yours: if you think I come hither as a lion, it were pity of my life. No, I am no such thing: I am a man as other men are'; and there indeed let him name his name, and tell them plainly he is Snug the joiner.

Quince

45   Well, it shall be so. But there is two hard things:

---

15   *Not a whit*: not at all.

15–16   *Write me*: write (here 'me' means nothing more than that the speaker has a keen interest in the subject).

19   *more better.* The double comparative was a common grammatical construction, used to give emphasis; it is not a sign of Bottom's ignorance.

23   *eight and six*: alternating lines of eight and six syllables—a common ballad metre (see Bottom's song, later in this scene, lines 112ff).

wants @ Quince to write a prolog so as not to scare women — realy wants more roles

33   *defect*: Bottom means 'effect'.

42   *it were . . . life*: my life would be in danger (he would have to ask for pity).

that is, to bring the moonlight into a chamber; for,
you know, Pyramus and Thisbe meet by moonlight.

Snout

Doth the moon shine that night we play our play?

Bottom

50 A calendar, a calendar! Look in the almanac; find
out moonshine, find out moonshine.

Quince

Yes, it doth shine that night.

Bottom

Why, then may you leave a casement of the great
chamber window, where we play, open; and the
55 moon may shine in at the casement.

Quince

Ay; or else one must come in with a bush of thorns
and a lantern, and say he comes to disfigure or to
present the person of Moonshine. Then there is
another thing: we must have a wall in the great
60 chamber; for Pyramus and Thisbe, says the story,
did talk through the chink of a wall.

Snug

You can never bring in a wall. What say you,
Bottom?

Bottom

Some man or other must present Wall; and let him
65 have some plaster, or some loam, or some rough-
cast about him, to signify wall; and let him hold his
fingers thus, and through that cranny shall Pyramus
and Thisbe whisper.

Quince

If that may be, then all is well. Come sit down,
70 every mother's son, and rehearse your parts.
Pyramus, you begin. When you have spoken your
speech, enter into that brake; and so every one
according to his cue.

Enter Puck

Puck

What hempen homespuns have we swaggering
here,
75 So near the cradle of the fairy queen?
What, a play toward? I'll be an auditor—
An actor too, perhaps, if I see cause.

53   *casement* : window.

57   *disfigure* : Quince means 'figure'
(=represent).
58   *the person of Moonshine.* The folk-
lore of many countries claims that there
is a man in the moon. Sometimes he is
said to be the man who broke the
Jewish sabbath laws by gathering
sticks and was punished by being
stoned to death (Book of Numbers
15:32–6). The 'bush of thorns'
represents the forbidden sticks, but
the dog referred to in *Act 5*, scene 1
seems to be Shakespeare's own
invention; he refers to the dog in the
moon in another play, *The Tempest*.
65   *loam* : mixture of clay, sand and
straw—used for making bricks.
65–6   *rough-cast* : mixture of lime and
gravel—used for plastering outside
walls of houses.
70   *every mother's son* : all of you.
72   *that brake* : the 'hawthorn-brake'
mentioned in line 4, which served as
green-room.
74   *hempen homespuns* : coarse country
folk (wearing homespun clothes made
of hemp).
76   *toward* : in preparation.
auditor : member of the audience.

Quince

Speak, Pyramus! Thisbe, stand forth.

Bottom

Thisbe, the flowers of odious savours sweet—

79 *odious* : hateful.

Quince

80 Odorous, odorous!

Bottom

savours : perfumes.

—odours savours sweet :
So hath thy breath my dearest Thisbe dear.
But hark, a voice! Stay thou but here awhile,
And by and by I will to thee appear.   [*Exit*

Puck

85 A stranger Pyramus than e'er play'd here!   [*Exit*

Flute

Must I speak now?

Quince

87 *marry* : by the Virgin Mary.

Ay, marry, must you; for you must understand, he
goes but to see a noise that he heard, and is to come
again.

Flute

90 *Most radiant Pyramus, most lily-white of hue,*
   Of colour like the red rose on triumphant brier,
Most brisky juvenal, and eke most lovely Jew,
   As true as truest horse that yet would never tire,
I'll meet thee, Pyramus, at Ninny's tomb.

92   It is impossible (and unnecessary)
to make sense out of this line.
Shakespeare formed 'brisky' from
'brisk' (just as 'frisky' is formed from
'frisk'); 'juvenal' may be a reference to
the Latin satirist, Juvenal—or Flute's
mispronunciation of 'juvenile'
(=young man). 'Jew' is needed only to
rhyme with 'hue'.

95   *Ninus* : king of Nineveh. Flute
comically mispronounces the name in
line 94; a 'ninny' is a fool.

Quince

95 'Ninus' tomb', man! Why, you must not speak that
yet; that you answer to Pyramus. You speak all
your part at once, cues and all. Pyramus, enter:
your cue is past; it is 'never tire'.

Flute

O!—*As true as truest horse, that yet would never tire.*

Enter Puck, *and* Bottom *wearing the ass's*
head.

Bottom

100 *fair* : handsome.
    were : would be.

100 *If I were fair, Thisbe, I were only thine.*

Quince

O monstrous! O strange! We are haunted! Pray,
masters! Fly, masters!—Help!

                    [*Exeunt all except* Bottom *and* Puck

Puck

103 *about a round* : roundabout.

I'll follow you, I'll lead you about a round,

106   *a fire :* a will-o'-the-wisp—the dancing light that appears over marshy ground, caused by the marsh gases.

109   *knavery :* trick.

115   *translated :* transformed.

120   *that :* so that.
121   *ousel-cock :* male blackbird (which has a dark yellow beak—'orange-tawny bill').
123   *throstle :* thrush.
124   *little quill :* shrill voice.
129–30 The cuckoo repeats two notes, sounding like 'cuck' and 'oo', which can be heard as 'cuckold'; this is the name given to a man whose wife is unfaithful to him. Very many ('full many') married men listen to ('mark') the cuckoo's song, and dare not deny that they are cuckolds.

131   *set his wit to :* use his intelligence against.

Through bog, through bush, through brake, through brier:
105   Sometime a horse I'll be, sometime a hound,
A hog, a headless bear, sometime a fire;
And neigh, and bark, and grunt, and roar, and burn,
Like horse, hound, hog, bear, fire, at every turn.
                                                    [*Exit*

Bottom
Why do they run away? This is a knavery of them to
110 make me afeard.

Enter Snout

Snout
O Bottom, thou art changed! What do I see on thee?

Bottom
What do you see? You see an ass-head of your own, do you?   [*Exit* Snout

Enter Quince

Quince
115 Bless thee, Bottom! Bless thee! Thou art translated.   [*Exit*

Bottom
I see their knavery! This is to make an ass of me; to
fright me, if they could. But I will not stir from this
place, do what they can: I will walk up and down
120 here, and I will sing, that they shall hear I am not
afraid.
The ousel-cock, so black of hue,
    With orange-tawny bill,
The throstle with his note so true,
125   The wren with little quill—
Titania   [*Waking*]
What angel wakes me from my flow'ry bed?
Bottom
The finch, the sparrow, and the lark,
    The plain-song cuckoo gray,
Whose note full many a man doth mark,
130   And dares not answer 'Nay'—
—for indeed, who would set his wit to so foolish a

132 *give . . . lie :* tell a bird that it is
lying.
133 *never so :* ever so much.

135 *note :* melody.
136 *enthralled to :* taken prisoner by.
shape : appearance.
137 *thy fair virtue's force :* the power
of your fine personality.
perforce : naturally.
move : persuade.
138 *On the first view :* at first sight.

143 *gleek :* make acute (even satiric)
observations.

146 *to serve . . . turn :* for my purpose.

149 *no common rate :* no ordinary rank.
150 *still :* always.
tend : attend.

bird? Who would give a bird the lie, though he cry
'cuckoo' never so?
Titania
I pray thee, gentle mortal, sing again!
135 Mine ear is much enamour'd of thy note;
So is mine eye enthralled to thy shape;
And thy fair virtue's force perforce doth move me
On the first view to say, to swear, I love thee.
Bottom
Methinks, mistress, you should have little reason
140 for that. And yet, to say the truth, reason and love
keep little company together nowadays—the more
the pity, that some honest neighbours will not make
them friends. Nay, I can gleek upon occasion.
Titania
Thou art as wise as thou art beautiful.
Bottom
145 Not so, neither; but if I had wit enough to get out of
this wood, I have enough to serve mine own turn.
Titania
Out of this wood do not desire to go:
Thou shalt remain here, whether thou wilt or no.
I am a spirit of no common rate;
150 The summer still doth tend upon my state;
And I do love thee; therefore go with me.
I'll give thee fairies to attend on thee,
And they shall fetch thee jewels from the deep,
And sing, while thou on pressed flowers dost sleep:
155 And I will purge thy mortal grossness so
That thou shalt like an airy spirit go.
Peaseblossom, Cobweb, Moth, and Mustardseed!

Enter four Fairies

Peaseblossom   Ready.

Cobweb   And I.

Moth   And I.

Mustardseed   And I.

All Four   Where shall we go?

160   *in his walks :* where he walks.
 gambol : romp.
 in his eyes : in his sight.
161   *apricocks :* an old form of
 'apricots'.
 dewberries : blackberries.
163   *humble-bees :* bumble-bees.
164   *night-tapers :* candles (for use at
 night).
 crop . . . thighs : trim the wax from
 the bees' legs.
165   *glow-worms' eyes :* the light, which
 shines like an eye, is actually in the
 glow-worm's tail.
166   *To have :* to attend.
169   *do him courtesies :* pay him
 homage.

174   *I . . . mercy :* I beg your pardon.

177   *I . . . acquaintance :* the polite
 formula spoken when first introduced
 to a stranger.
178   *if . . . finger :* cobwebs (spiders'
 webs) were used to cover a bleeding
 cut.
178–9 *make bold with :* take advantage of.
180   *Peaseblossom :* the flower of the
 pea plant.
181   *Squash :* an unripe pea-pod.
182   *Peascod :* a ripe pea-pod.

185   *Mustardseed :* mustard is used as a
 sharp sauce to eat with roast beef.
186–90 Bottom pretends to sympathize
 with Mustardseed because many of his
 family ('house') have been eaten.

Titania
Be kind and courteous to this gentleman:
160 Hop in his walks, and gambol in his eyes;
Feed him with apricocks and dewberries,
With purple grapes, green figs, and mulberries.
The honey-bags steal from the humble-bees,
And for night-tapers crop their waxen thighs,
165 And light them at the fiery glow-worms' eyes,
To have my love to bed, and to arise.
And pluck the wings from painted butterflies
To fan the moonbeams from his sleeping eyes.
Nod to him, elves, and do him courtesies.
 Peaseblossom
170 Hail, mortal!
 Cobweb
Hail!
 Moth
Hail!
 Mustardseed
Hail!
 Bottom
I cry your worships mercy, heartily. I beseech your
175 worship's name?
 Cobweb
Cobweb.
 Bottom
I shall desire you of more acquaintance, good
Master Cobweb: if I cut my finger, I shall make
bold with you. Your name, honest gentleman?
 Peaseblossom
180 Peaseblossom.
 Bottom
I pray you, commend me to Mistress Squash, your
mother, and to Master Peascod, your father. Good
Master Peaseblossom, I shall desire you of more
acquaintance too. Your name, I beseech you, sir?
 Mustardseed
185 Mustardseed.
 Bottom
Good Master Mustardseed, I know your patience
well: that same cowardly, giant-like ox-beef hath
devoured many a gentleman of your house. I
promise you, your kindred hath made my eyes

190   *ere* : before.

190 water ere now. I desire your more acquaintance,
    good Master Mustardseed.
                Titania
    Come, wait upon him; lead him to my bower.
    The moon, methinks, looks with a watery eye;
    And when she weeps, weeps every little flower,
195 Lamenting some enforced chastity.
    Tie up my love's tongue, bring him silently.

                                    [*Exeunt*

194–5   The Elizabethans believed that
    dew fell from the moon on to the
    flowers, which looked as though they
    were weeping; Titania suggests that
    the flowers grieve because their
    chastity has been violated ('enforced').

Scene 2 *Another part of the wood*

                Enter Oberon

            Oberon
    I wonder if Titania be awak'd;
    Then, what it was that next came in her eye,
    Which she must dote on in extremity?
    Here comes my messenger.

                Enter Puck

                            How now, mad spirit?
5 What night-rule now about this haunted grove?
            Puck
    My mistress with a monster is in love!
    Near to her close and consecrated bower,
    While she was in her dull and sleeping hour,
    A crew of patches, rude mechanicals,
10 That work for bread upon Athenian stalls,
    Were met together to rehearse a play
    Intended for great Theseus' nuptial day.
    The shallowest thick-skin of that barren sort,
    Who Pyramus presented in their sport,
15 Forsook his scene and enter'd in a brake,
    When I did him at this advantage take:
    An ass's nole I fixed on his head.
    Anon his Thisbe must be answered,
    And forth my mimic comes. When they him spy,
20 As wild geese that the creeping fowler eye,
    Or russet-pated choughs, many in sort,
    Rising and cawing at the gun's report,
    Sever themselves, and madly sweep the sky;
    So at his sight away his fellows fly,

Act 3   Scene 2
Oberon discovers Puck's mistake. He
has put the love-juice on the wrong
man's eyes. Demetrius is still in love
with Hermia, but Lysander (through
the effect of the juice) has fallen in love
with Helena. Hermia is searching for
Lysander. She leaves Demetrius, who
falls asleep, giving Oberon the
opportunity to put love-juice on *his*
eyes. When Demetrius wakes and sees
Helena, he declares his passion for her.
The four lovers all join in a quarrel,
and the men are preparing to fight a
duel. But Oberon instructs Puck to
mislead them, so that they cannot
harm each other. Finally, each lover is
brought back to the stage where (not
knowing the presence of the others)
they all lie down to sleep. Puck anoints
their eyes again, making sure that this
time Demetrius will fall in love with
Helena, and Lysander will once again
be in love with Hermia.

1   *be awak'd* : has woken up.
2   *eye* : sight.
3   *in extremity* : excessively.
5   *night-rule* : business of the night.
7   *close* : secret.
8   *dull* : drowsy.
      patches : clowns.
      rude : rough.
      mechanicals : workmen.
10   *stalls* : shops in the market.
13   *shallowest* : most stupid.
      thick-skin : numskull (person
incapable of sensitive feelings).
      barren : unimaginative.
      sort : crowd.

14   *Who . . . presented* : who acted the part of Pyramus.

15   *Forsook his scene* : left the stage.
      brake : bush.

17   *nole* : headpiece.

18   *Anon* : presently.

19   *mimic* : comedian.

20   *fowler* : hunter.
      eye : perceive.

21   *russet-pated choughs* : grey-headed jackdaws.
      many in sort : in a large flock.

23   *Sever* : separate.

24   *at his sight* : at the sight of him.

25   *at our stamp* : when I gave the signal (by stamping on the ground).

26   *He* : one man.

27   *lost with* : conquered by.

28   *senseless things* : inanimate objects.
      wrong : injury.

30   *from . . . catch* : everything steals from those who surrender.

32   *translated* : transformed.

36   *latch'd* : moistened.

38   *took* : caught.

40   *That* : so that.
      of force : necessarily.
      ey'd : seen.

41   *close* : hidden.

44   *Lay breath* : use words.

48   Since you have already stepped into blood (as into shallow water), go on into the depths.

53–4 A hole could be drilled through the solid ('whole') earth so that the moon could creep through the middle and shine at midday in the Antipodes, thus annoying (disturbing) her brother, the sun.

54   *displease* : disturb.
      Her brother : the sun.

57   *dead* : deadly.

25   And, at our stamp, here o'er and o'er one falls;
      He 'Murder!' cries, and help from Athens calls.
      Their sense thus weak, lost with their fears thus strong,
      Made senseless things begin to do them wrong;
      For briers and thorns at their apparel snatch;
30   Some sleeves, some hats; from yielders all things catch.
      I led them on in this distracted fear,
      And left sweet Pyramus translated there;
      When in that moment, so it came to pass,
      Titania wak'd, and straightway lov'd an ass.

Oberon
35   This falls out better than I could devise!
      But hast thou yet latch'd the Athenian's eyes
      With the love-juice, as I did bid thee do?

Puck
      I took him sleeping—that is finish'd too;
      And the Athenian woman by his side;
40   That, when he wak'd, of force she must be ey'd.

Enter Demetrius *and* Hermia

Oberon
      Stand close: this is the same Athenian.

Puck
      This is the woman; but not this the man.

Demetrius
      O why rebuke you him that loves you so?
      Lay breath so bitter on your bitter foe.

Hermia
45   Now I but chide; but I should use thee worse,
      For thou, I fear, hast given me cause to curse.
      If thou hast slain Lysander in his sleep,
      Being o'er shoes in blood, plunge in the deep,
      And kill me too.
50   The sun was not so true unto the day
      As he to me. Would he have stol'n away
      From sleeping Hermia? I'll believe as soon
      This whole earth may be bor'd, and that the moon
      May through the centre creep, and so displease
55   Her brother's noontide with th' Antipodes.
      It cannot be but thou hast murder'd him;
      So should a murderer look, so dead, so grim.

Demetrius
So should the murder'd look, and so should I,
Pierc'd through the heart with your stern cruelty.
60 Yet you, the murderer, look as bright, as clear,
As yonder Venus in her glimmering sphere.

Hermia
What's this to my Lysander? Where is he?
Ah, good Demetrius, wilt thou give him me?

Demetrius
I had rather give his carcass to my hounds.

Hermia
65 Out, dog! out, cur! Thou driv'st me past the bounds
Of maiden's patience. Hast thou slain him then?
Henceforth be never number'd among men!
O once tell true—tell true, e'en for my sake;
Durst thou have look'd upon him being awake,
70 And hast thou kill'd him sleeping? O brave touch!
Could not a worm, an adder, do so much?
An adder did it; for with doubler tongue
Than thine, thou serpent, never adder stung.

Demetrius
You spend your passion on a mispris'd mood:
75 I am not guilty of Lysander's blood,
Nor is he dead, for aught that I can tell.

Hermia
I pray thee, tell me then that he is well.

Demetrius
An if I could, what should I get therefor?

Hermia
A privilege—never to see me more.
80 And from thy hated presence part I so;
See me no more, whe'r he be dead or no.   [*Exit*

Demetrius
There is no following her in this fierce vein:
Here therefore for a while I will remain.
So sorrow's heaviness doth heavier grow
85 For debt that bankrupt sleep doth sorrow owe,
Which now in some slight measure it will pay,
If for his tender here I make some stay.

[*Lies down and sleeps*

61 *Venus*: the planet.
 sphere: orbit.
62 *to*: to do with.

67 *number'd ... men*: counted as a man.
68 *once tell true*: speak the truth once and for all.
 e'en: even.
69 *Durst*: dare.
71 *worm*: snake.
72 *adder*: the adder has a forked tongue, the emblem of deceit.
74 *spend*: waste.
 on ... mood: in a mistaken anger.
76 *aught*: anything.

78 *An if*: if indeed.
 therefor: for that.
81 *whe'r*: whether.
82 *no following*: no point in following.
 vein: temper.
84–5 The fatigue ('heaviness') caused by sorrow becomes worse through lack of sleep—which is caused by sorrow.
85–7 Although Sleep is unable to recompense Demetrius fully (because it is 'bankrupt'), it will pay a little ('some slight measure') of the debt it owes him [i.e. the sleep he has lost through sorrow] if he will wait ('make some stay') for what it has to offer ('tender').

88   *quite* : completely.
89   *true love* : true lover.
90   *misprision* : mistake.
      perforce : inevitably.
91   *true love turn'd* : true love turned false.
92   If so, then fate takes charge, so that whilst one man keeps his word (holds troth), a million break ('fail') their promises, breaking one vow after another.

96   *fancy-sick* : love-sick.
      cheer : complexion.
97   The Elizabethans believed that every sigh wasted a drop of blood.
98   *illusion* : trick.
99   *against . . . appear* : in preparation for when she comes.
101   *Tartar.* The Tartars were notorious warriors (from central Asia), who fought with bows and arrows.
102   *dye* : colour.

104   *apple* : pupil.

108   *by* : near.
109   *remedy* : cure (for love's wound).

113   *lover's fee* : return (repayment) of love.
114   *fond* : foolish.
      pageant : exhibition.

118   *at once* : at the same time.
119   That in itself ('alone') is bound to be amusing.

Oberon
What hast thou done? Thou hast mistaken quite,
And laid the love-juice on some true love's sight:
90 Of thy misprision must perforce ensue
Some true love turn'd, and not a false turn'd true.
   Puck
Then fate o'er-rules, that, one man holding troth,
A million fail, confounding oath on oath.
   Oberon
About the wood go swifter than the wind,
95 And Helena of Athens look thou find:
All fancy-sick she is, and pale of cheer
With sighs of love, that costs the fresh blood dear.
By some illusion see thou bring her here.
I'll charm his eyes against she do appear.
   Puck
100 I go, I go—look how I go—
Swifter than arrow from the Tartar's bow.   [*Exit*
   Oberon
            Flower of this purple dye,
            Hit with Cupid's archery,
            Sink in apple of his eye.
               [*Squeezes the flower on* Demetrius' *eyes*]
105   When his love he doth espy,
            Let her shine as gloriously
            As the Venus of the sky.
            When thou wak'st, if she be by,
            Beg of her for remedy.

            Enter Puck

   Puck
110   Captain of our fairy band,
            Helena is here at hand
            And the youth, mistook by me,
            Pleading for a lover's fee.
            Shall we their fond pageant see?
115   Lord, what fools these mortals be!
   Oberon
Stand aside. The noise they make
Will cause Demetrius to awake.
   Puck
Then will two at once woo one;
That must needs be sport alone;

121 *befall :* happen.
  preposterously : extraordinarily.
124–5 *vows . . . appears :* vows which are born (first spoken) in tears show from their birth that they are genuine.
126–7 How can my qualities (e.g. his love) appear despicable ('scorn') since they bear my tears, which are like badges (worn by servants, or members of a society, to indicate their loyalty).
128 *advance :* display.
129 *truth kills truth :* the true love that Lysander swears to Helena destroys the other true love that he swore to Hermia. The fight ('fray') between the two truths is both 'devilish' (because truth is being destroyed) and 'holy' (because truth is the victor).
130 *give her o'er :* renounce your love for here.
131 *Weigh . . . oath :* balance the oaths sworn to Hermia against those that he is swearing to Helena.
  nothing weigh : 'there will be no difference between the weights'; and also 'there is no weight (=value) in the oaths.'

133 *tales :* fictions, falsehoods.
138 *eyne :* eyes.
139 *show :* appearance.
141 *Taurus :* a mountain range in Asia Minor.
144 *princess . . . white :* sovereign whiteness.
  seal : if Helena gives him her hand as a token of marriage, it will seal (=make official) his happiness.
145 *bent :* determined.
146 *set against :* attack.
150 *in souls :* in intention.

120 And those things do best please me
That befall preposterously.

Enter Lysander *and* Helena

Lysander
Why should you think that I should woo in scorn?
Scorn and derision never come in tears:
Look, when I vow, I weep; and vows so born,
125 In their nativity all truth appears.
How can these things in me seem scorn to you,
Bearing the badge of faith to prove them true?
Helena
You do advance your cunning more and more.
When truth kills truth, O devilish-holy fray!
130 These vows are Hermia's: will you give her o'er?
Weigh oath with oath, and you will nothing weigh:
Your vows, to her and me, put in two scales,
Will even weigh, and both as light as tales.
Lysander
I had no judgement when to her I swore.
Helena
135 Nor none, in my mind, now you give her o'er.
Lysander
Demetrius loves her, and he loves not you.
Demetrius   [*Waking*]
O Helen, goddess, nymph, perfect, divine!
To what, my love, shall I compare thine eyne?
Crystal is muddy. O how ripe in show
140 Thy lips, those kissing cherries, tempting grow;
That pure congealed white, high Taurus' snow,
Fann'd with the eastern wind, turns to a crow
When thou hold'st up thy hand. O let me kiss
This princess of pure white, this seal of bliss.
Helena
145 O spite! O hell! I see you all are bent
To set against me for your merriment.
If you were civil and knew courtesy,
You would not do me thus much injury.
Can you not hate me, as I know you do,
150 But you must join in souls to mock me too?

151   *show :* appearance.

153   *superpraise :* praise with
    superlatives.
    parts : qualities.

157   *trim :* fine.

159   *sort :* birth.
160   *extort :* torment.

168   *idle :* useless.

169   *I will none :* I will have nothing to
    do with her.

171   My heart was only visiting her,
    like a guest.

175   *aby it dear :* pay dearly for it.

177   *that . . . takes :* that deprives the
    sight of its ability.
178   Makes the ear quicker to catch
    sounds.
179–80   When the sense of sight is
    damaged, the hearing, in
    compensation, is made twice as strong.
182   *thy sound :* the sound of your
    voice.
184   *press :* urge.

If you were men, as men you are in show,
You would not use a gentle lady so;
To vow, and swear, and superpraise my parts,
When I am sure you hate me with your hearts.
155 You both are rivals, and love Hermia,
And now both rivals, to mock Helena.
A trim exploit, a manly enterprise,
To conjure tears up in a poor maid's eyes
With your derision! None of noble sort
160 Would so offend a virgin, and extort
A poor soul's patience, all to make you sport.
    Lysander
You are unkind, Demetrius. Be not so;
For you love Hermia—this you know I know.
And here, with all good will, with all my heart,
165 In Hermia's love I yield you up my part;
And yours of Helena to me bequeath,
Whom I do love, and will do to my death.
    Helena
Never did mockers waste more idle breath.
    Demetrius
Lysander, keep thy Hermia; I will none:
170 If e'er I lov'd her, all that love is gone.
My heart to her but as guest-wise sojourn'd,
And now to Helen is it home return'd,
There to remain.
    Lysander   Helen, it is not so.
    Demetrius
Disparage not the faith thou dost not know,
175 Lest to thy peril thou aby it dear.
Look where thy love comes: yonder is thy dear.

Enter Hermia

    Hermia
Dark night, that from the eye his function takes,
The ear more quick of apprehension makes;
Wherein it doth impair the seeing sense,
180 It pays the hearing double recompense.
Thou art not by mine eye, Lysander, found;
Mine ear, I thank it, brought me to thy sound.
But why unkindly didst thou leave me so?
    Lysander
Why should he stay, whom love doth press to go?

Hermia

185 What love could press Lysander from my side?

Lysander

Lysander's love, that would not let him bide,
Fair Helena, who more engilds the night
Than all yon fiery oes and eyes of light.
Why seek'st thou me? Could not this make thee know,

190 The hate I bare thee made me leave thee so?

Hermia

You speak not as you think: it cannot be.

Helena

Lo, she is one of this confederacy!
Now I perceive they have conjoin'd all three
To fashion this false sport in spite of me.

195 Injurious Hermia, most ungrateful maid!
Have you conspir'd, have you with these contriv'd
To bait me with this foul derision?
Is all the counsel that we two have shar'd—
The sisters' vows, the hours that we have spent,

200 When we have chid the hasty-footed time
For parting us—O, is all forgot?
All school-days' friendship, childhood innocence?
We, Hermia, like two artificial gods,
Have with our needles created both one flower,

205 Both on one sampler, sitting on one cushion,
Both warbling of one song, both in one key,
As if our hands, our sides, voices, and minds,
Had been incorporate. So we grew together,
Like to a double cherry, seeming parted,

210 But yet a union in partition,
Two lovely berries moulded on one stem;
So, with two seeming bodies, but one heart;

186   *bide* : stay.
187   *engilds* : lights up.
188   *yon* : yonder.
  oes : orbs; the 'oes and eyes of light'
are the stars.

190   *bare* : felt towards.

193   *conjoin'd* : joined together.
194   *in spite* : to vex.
195   *Injurious* : insulting.
196   *contriv'd* : plotted.
197   *bait* : torment (Helena sees herself
as the bear which was baited with dogs
to provide entertainment).
198   *counsel* : confidences.
199   *sisters' vows* : promises to be sisters
to each other.
200   *chid* : reproached.
203   *artificial gods* : gods with skill in
creative art.
204   *needle* : the word was often
pronounced 'neele'.
205   *sampler* : piece of embroidery.

208   *incorporate* : of a single body.

210   Still joined together, although
separate.
212   *with . . . heart* : apparently with
two bodies, but with one heart.

BEAR-BAITING

213–4   Helena uses a complicated image from heraldry to describe her relationship with Hermia. Medieval knights carried on their shields different devices by which they could easily be identified; these were called 'coats of arms' ('coats in heraldry'), and were later adopted by noble families, universities, schools, and other institutions. When a knight married a lady of noble family, his coat of arms was combined with hers to make a new coat, usually in the shape of a shield. Above the shield was placed ('crowned' is the technical term) a 'crest' (such as a plume or helmet) to signify the union. Soon after he wrote this play, Shakespeare was granted his own coat of arms.

214   *Due but to one:* belonging only to one.
215   *rent:* tear.
      ancient: former.
      asunder: apart.
225   *even but now:* very recently.
227   *Wherefore:* for what reason?
229   *your love:* his love for you.
230   *tender:* offer.
      forsooth: indeed.
231   *setting on:* incitement.
232   *grace:* favour.
237   *persever:* carry on (stressed perséver).
      sad looks: solemn faces.
238   *Make mouths upon:* pull faces at.
239   *hold . . . up:* keep up the game.
240   *carried:* performed.
      chronicled: recorded as history.
242   *argument:* object of ridicule.

Two of the first, like coats in heraldry,
Due but to one, and crowned with one crest.
215 And will you rent our ancient love asunder,
To join with men in scorning your poor friend?
It is not friendly, 'tis not maidenly:
Our sex, as well as I, may chide you for it,
Though I alone do feel the injury.
     Hermia
220 I am amazed at your passionate words.
I scorn you not: it seems that you scorn me.
     Helena
Have you not set Lysander, as in scorn,
To follow me and praise my eyes and face,
And made your other love, Demetrius—
225 Who even but now did spurn me with his foot—
To call me goddess, nymph, divine and rare,
Precious, celestial? Wherefore speaks he this
To her he hates? And wherefore doth Lysander
Deny your love, so rich within his soul,
230 And tender me, forsooth, affection,
But by your setting on, by your consent?
What though I be not so in grace as you,
So hung upon with love, so fortunate,
But miserable most, to love unlov'd?
235 This you should pity rather than despise.
     Hermia
I understand not what you mean by this.
     Helena
Ay, do, persever, counterfeit sad looks,
Make mouths upon me when I turn my back,
Wink each at other, hold the sweet jest up.
240 This sport, well carried, shall be chronicled.
If you have any pity, grace, or manners,
You would not make me such an argument.
But fare ye well: 'tis partly mine own fault,
Which death or absence soon shall remedy.
     Lysander
245 Stay, gentle Helena! Hear my excuse:
My love, my life, my soul, fair Helena!
     Helena
O excellent!
     Hermia   Sweet, do not scorn her so.

Demetrius
If she cannot entreat, I can compel.
Lysander
Thou canst compel no more than she entreat.
250 Thy threats have no more strength than her weak
   prayers.
Helen, I love thee; by my life, I do.
I swear by that which I will lose for thee.
To prove him false that says I love thee not.
Demetrius
I say I love thee more than he can do.
Lysander
255 If thou say so, withdraw, and prove it too.
Demetrius
Quick, come!
Hermia   Lysander, whereto tends all this?

Lysander
Away, you Ethiope!
Demetrius   No, no! He'll seem
To break loose; take on, as you would follow,
But yet come not: you are a tame man, go!
Lysander   [*To* Hermia]
260 Hang off, thou cat, thou burr! Vile thing, let loose,
Or I will shake thee from me like a serpent.
Hermia
Why are you grown so rude? What change is this,
Sweet love?
Lysander   Thy love! Out, tawny Tartar, out!
Out, loathed medicine! Hated potion, hence!
Hermia
265 Do you not jest?
Helena   Yes, sooth; and so do you.
Lysander
Demetrius, I will keep my word with thee.
Demetrius
I would I had your bond, for I perceive
A weak bond holds you: I'll not trust your word.
Lysander
What, should I hurt her, strike her, kill her dead?
270 Although I hate her, I'll not harm her so.
Hermia
What, can you do me greater harm than hate?

255 *withdraw :* come outside.
prove it : i.e. by fighting a duel.

256 *whereto . . . this :* what does this mean?

257 *Ethiope :* Lysander intends to insult Hermia because of her dark complexion.
258 *take on :* pretend.
259 *tame :* spiritless.

260 *burr :* the prickly seed-head of the burdock plant: it catches on clothes and is very difficult to shake off.
264 *tawny Tartar :* Lysander again insults Hermia for the colour of her skin, and also for the fiery temper which he associates with the Tartars (see note to line 101).

265 *sooth :* indeed.

267 *bond :* signed contract; in the next line Demetrius uses another sense of the word.
268 *bond :* chain (i.e. Hermia's arms).

272   *what news* : what does this mean.

274   *erewhile* : a short time ago.
275   *Since night* : since night fell.

277   *In earnest* : seriously (not as a joke).

282   *juggler* : trickster.
canker-blossom : worm that eats away the flower (or perhaps 'worm-eaten flower').

290   *compare* : comparison.
291   *urg'd her height* : argued that her height makes her attractive.

296   *painted* : Hermia implies that Helena's complexion is the result of cosmetics (generally disapproved of by the Elizabethans).
maypole : a tall pole, erected on the village green for the traditional May dances.

Hate me! Wherefore? O me, what news, my love?
Am not I Hermia? Are not you Lysander?
I am as fair now as I was erewhile.
275 Since night you lov'd me; yet, since night you left
         me:
Why, then you left me—O the gods forbid!—
In earnest, shall I say?
          Lysander   Ay, by my life;
And never did desire to see thee more.
Therefore be out of hope, of question, of doubt;
280 Be certain, nothing truer: 'tis no jest,
That I do hate thee and love Helena.
          Hermia
O me! You juggler, you canker-blossom,
You thief of love! What, have you come by night
And stol'n my love's heart from him?
          Helena   Fine, i' faith!
285 Have you no modesty, no maiden shame,
No touch of bashfulness? What, will you tear
Impatient answers from my gentle tongue?
Fie, Fie, you counterfeit, you puppet you!
          Hermia
Puppet! Why, so: ay, that way goes the game.
290 Now I perceive that she hath made compare
Between our statures: she hath urg'd her height;
And with her personage, her tall personage,
Her height, forsooth, she hath prevail'd with him.
And are you grown so high in his esteem,
295 Because I am so dwarfish and so low?
How low am I, thou painted maypole? Speak!

How low am I? I am not yet so low
But that my nails can reach unto thine eyes.
   Helena
I pray you, though you mock me, gentlemen,

300 | 300   Let her not hurt me. I was never curst;
301   *shrewishness :* quarrelling. | I have no gift at all in shrewishness;
302   *right :* true. | I am a right maid for my cowardice:

300   *curst :* bad-tempered.
301   *shrewishness :* quarrelling.
302   *right :* true.

300   Let her not hurt me. I was never curst;
I have no gift at all in shrewishness;
I am a right maid for my cowardice:
Let her not strike me. You perhaps may think,
Because she is something lower than myself,
305   That I can match her. . . .
   Hermia   'Lower'! Hark, again!
   Helena
Good Hermia, do not be so bitter with me.
I evermore did love you, Hermia,

308   *counsels :* secrets.
310   *stealth :* secret flight.
312   *chid me hence :* ordered me to go away from here.
314   *so :* provided that.
      quiet : peacefully.
317   *fond :* foolish.
323   *shrewd :* malicious.
324   *vixen :* the female fox is noted for its sharp attacks.

Did ever keep your counsels, never wronged you—
Save that, in love unto Demetrius,
310   I told him of your stealth unto this wood.
He follow'd you; for love I follow'd him;
But he hath chid me hence, and threaten'd me
To strike me, spurn me—nay, to kill me too.
And now, so you will let me quiet go,
315   To Athens will I bear my folly back,
And follow you no further. Let me go:
You see how simple and how fond I am.
   Hermia
Why, get you gone. Who is't that hinders you?
   Helena
A foolish heart that I leave here behind.
   Hermia
What, with Lysander?
320   **Helena**   With Demetrius.
   Lysander
Be not afraid: she shall not harm thee, Helena.
   Demetrius
No, sir; she shall not, though you take her part.
   Helena
O, when she's angry, she is keen and shrewd.
She was a vixen when she went to school:

325   *but :* only.
327   *flout :* mock.
328   *minimus :* the smallest of all creatures.
      knot-grass : a low-growing weed with creeping stems.

325   And though she be but little, she is fierce.
   Hermia
'Little' again! Nothing but 'low' and 'little'!
Why will you suffer her to flout me thus?
Let me come to her.

Lysander   Get you gone, you dwarf;
You minimus, of hindering knot-grass made;
330 You bead, you acorn!
Demetrius   You are too officious
In her behalf that scorns your services.
Let her alone. Speak not of Helena.
Take not her part; for if thou dost intend
Never so little show of love to her,
335 Thou shalt aby it.
Lysander   Now she holds me not.
Now follow, if thou dar'st, to try whose right,
Of thine or mine, is most in Helena.
Demetrius
Follow! Nay, I'll go with thee, cheek by jowl.
    [*Exeunt* Lysander *and* Demetrius
Hermia
You, mistress, all this coil is 'long of you:
340 Nay, go not back.
Helena   I will not trust you, I,
Nor longer stay in your curst company.
Your hands than mine are quicker for a fray,
My legs are longer though, to run away.   [*Exit*
Hermia
I am amaz'd, and know not what to say.   [*Exit*
Oberon
345 This is thy negligence: still thou mistak'st,
Or else commit'st thy knaveries wilfully.
Puck
Believe me, king of shadows, I mistook.
Did not you tell me I should know the man
By the Athenian garments he had on?
350 And so far blameless proves my enterprise,
That I have 'nointed an Athenian's eyes;
And so far am I glad it so did sort,
As this their jangling I esteem a sport.
Oberon
Thou see'st these lovers seek a place to fight.
355 Hie therefore, Robin, overcast the night;
The starry welkin cover thou anon
With drooping fog as black as Acheron,
And lead these testy rivals so astray,
As one come not within another's way.
360 Like to Lysander sometime frame thy tongue,

330   *officious* : interfering.

333–4   *if . . . her* : if you pretend to show the least sign of love for her.

335   *aby it* : pay for it.

336   *try* : make trial (in a duel).

338   *cheek by jowl* : cheek by cheek (not one behind the other).

339   *coil* : trouble.
    'long of : on account of.

341   *curst* : bad-tempered.
342   *fray* : fight.

345   *still thou mistak'st* : you are always making mistakes.

352   *sort* : happen.
353   *jangling* : quarrelling.
    esteem a sport : consider a joke.
355   *Hie* : go.
    overcast : cover with clouds.
356   *welkin* : sky.
    anon : at once.
357   *Acheron* : a black river in the classical underworld.
358   *testy* : irritable.
360   *frame thy tongue* : make your voice sound.

361 *stir . . . up* : provoke.
362 *rail* : insult.

364 *death-counterfeiting sleep* : sleep
     that looks like death.
365 *batty* : bat-like.

367 *virtuous property* : powerful
     quality.
368 *his might* : its strength.
369 *wonted* : accustomed.
370 *derision* : delusion.
371 *fruitless* : meaningless.
372 *wend* : return.
373 *league* : union.
     whose . . . end : which will last as
     long as they live.
375 *I'll to* : I'll go to.

379 *full* : very.
380 *Aurora's harbinger* : the morning
     star (Phosphor) which heralded the
     approach of dawn (the goddess
     Aurora).
281-7 Puck distinguishes two kinds of
     ghost—those who merely wander away
     from the churchyards where their
     bodies are buried, and those who are
     damned because they are the spirits of
     men who committed suicide. The
     bodies of suicides were not buried in
     consecrated ground, but either
     remained in the rivers ('floods') where
     they had drowned themselves, or else
     were interred where two roads crossed
     ('cross-ways'). Since the suicides
     deliberately ('wilfully') deprived
     themselves of life ('light'), they are now
     condemned to keep company
     ('consort') only with the night.
389 *morning* : Aurora.
392 *Neptune* : god of the ocean.
395 *effect* : complete.

Then stir Demetrius up with bitter wrong;
And sometime rail thou like Demetrius;
And from each other look thou lead them thus,
Till o'er their brows death-counterfeiting sleep
365 With leaden legs and batty wings doth creep.
Then crush this herb into Lysander's eye—
Whose liquor hath this virtuous property,
To take from thence all error with his might,
And make his eyeballs roll with wonted sight.
370 When they next wake, all this derision
Shall seem a dream and fruitless vision;
And back to Athens shall the lovers wend,
With league whose date till death shall never end.
Whiles I in this affair do thee employ,
375 I'll to my queen and beg her Indian boy;
And then I will her charmed eye release
From monster's view, and all things shall be peace.
       Puck
My fairy lord, this must be done with haste,
For night's swift dragons cut the clouds full fast,
380 And yonder shines Aurora's harbinger;
At whose approach ghosts, wandering here and
    there,
Troop home to churchyards. Damned spirits all,
That in cross-ways and floods have burial,
Already to their wormy beds are gone,
385 For fear lest day should look their shames upon:
They wilfully themselves exil'd from light,
And must for aye consort with black-brow'd night.
       Oberon
But we are spirits of another sort.
I with the morning's love have oft made sport;
390 And like a forester the groves may tread,
Even till the eastern gate, all fiery red,
Opening on Neptune with fair blessed beams,
Turns into yellow gold his salt green streams.
But, notwithstanding, haste; make no delay:
395 We may effect this business yet ere day.   [*Exit*

       Puck
         Up and down, up and down,
         I will lead them up and down.
         I am fear'd in field and town;

Goblin, lead them up and down.
400 Here comes one.

Enter Lysander

Lysander
Where art thou, proud Demetrius? Speak thou
now.
Puck

402   *drawn :* with sword drawn.

Here, villain, drawn and ready. Where art thou?
Lysander
I will be with thee straight.

403   *straight :* straightaway,
immediately.
404   *plainer :* smoother.

Puck   Follow me, then,
To plainer ground.   [*Exit* Lysander

Enter Demetrius

Demetrius   Lysander, speak again.
405 Thou runaway, thou coward, art thou fled?
Speak! In some bush? Where dost thou hide thy
head?
Puck

407   *bragging :* boasting.

Thou coward, art thou bragging to the stars,
Telling the bushes that thou look'st for wars,

409   *recreant :* coward.

And wilt not come? Come, recreant; come, thou
child;

410   *defil'd :* dishonoured.

410 I'll whip thee with a rod: he is defil'd
That draws a sword on thee.
Demetrius   Yea, art thou there?
Puck

412   *try no manhood :* make no test of
courage.

Follow my voice: we'll try no manhood here.
                [*Exeunt*

Enter Lysander

Lysander
He goes before me and still dares me on:
When I come where he calls, then he is gone.

413   *still :* always.
    dares me on : challenges me to
follow.
414   *where :* to where.
415   *much lighter-heel'd :* moves far
more quickly.
417   *That :* with the result that.
    in : into.

415 The villain is much lighter-heel'd than I:
I follow'd fast, but faster he did fly,
That fallen am I in dark uneven way,
And here will rest me. [*Lies down*] Come, thou
gentle day!
For if but once thou show me thy grey light,
420 I'll find Demetrius and revenge this spite.
                [*Sleeps*

Enter Puck *and* Demetrius

Puck

Ho, ho, ho! Coward, why com'st thou not?

Demetrius

422 *Abide me :* wait for me.
    wot : know.

Abide me, if thou dar'st; for well I wot

423 *shifting . . . place :* always
    changing places.

Thou runn'st before me, shifting every place,
And dar'st not stand, nor look me in the face.

425 Where art thou now?

Puck   Come hither: I am here.

Demetrius

426 *buy this dear :* pay dearly for this.

Nay then, thou mock'st me. Thou shalt buy this
      dear
If ever I thy face by daylight see.

428 *constraineth :* compels.

Now, go thy way. Faintness constraineth me

429 *measure . . . length :* lie at full
    length.

To measure out my length on this cold bed:

430 *visited :* found out

430 By day's approach look to be visited.

[*Lies down and sleeps*

Enter Helena

Helena

O weary night! O long and tedious night,

432 *Abate :* shorten.

Abate thy hours. Shine comforts, from the east,
That I may back to Athens by daylight,

434 *my poor company :* the company of
    poor me.

From these that my poor company detest:

435 And sleep, that sometimes shuts up sorrow's eye,
Steal me awhile from mine own company.

[*Lies down and sleeps*

Puck

Yet but three? Come one more;
Two of both kinds makes up four.

439 *curst :* cross.

Here she comes, curst and sad:

440   Cupid is a knavish lad,
Thus to make poor females mad.

Enter Hermia

Hermia

Never so weary, never so in woe,
Bedabbled with the dew and torn with briers,

444 *go :* walk.

I can no further crawl, no further go;

445 My legs can keep no pace with my desires.
Here will I rest me till the break of day.

447 *mean a fray :* intend to fight.

Heavens shield Lysander, if they mean a fray!

[*Lies down and sleeps*

Puck
On the ground,
Sleep sound:
450   I'll apply
To your eye,
Gentle lover, remedy
    [*He squeezes the juice on* Lysander's *eyes*
When thou wak'st,
Thou tak'st
455   True delight
In the sight
Of thy former lady's eye:
And the country proverb known,
That every man should take his own,
460   In your waking shall be shown:
Jack shall have Jill;
Naught shall go ill;
The man shall have his mare again,
And all shall be well.   [*Exit*

461   *Jack . . . Jill:* a proverbial saying,
meaning that every man shall have his
woman.

Act 4

Scene 1 *The wood ;* Lysander, Demetrius, Hermia
and Helena *are sleeping*

> *Enter* Titania *and* Bottom *with* Fairies *in
> attendance ;* Oberon *follows*

Titania
Come, sit thee down upon this flow'ry bed,
While I thy amiable cheeks do coy,
And stick musk-roses in thy sleek, smooth head,
And kiss thy fair large ears, my gentle joy.

Bottom
5 Where's Peaseblossom?

Peaseblossom
Ready.

Bottom
Scratch my head, Peaseblossom. Where's Mounsieur Cobweb?

Cobweb
Ready.

Bottom
10 Mounsieur Cobweb, good Mounsieur, get you your
weapons in your hand, and kill me a red-hipped
humble-bee on the top of a thistle; and, good

13   *fret :* trouble.

16   *be loath :* hate.
      overflown : swamped.
17   *signior :* Bottom's
      mispronunciation of the Italian
      'signor'.

20   *neaf :* hand.
21   *leave your curtsy :* stop bowing to
      me.
22   *what's your will :* what would you
      like?
23   *Cavalery :* Bottom's attempt at the
      Italian 'cavaliere' (=English 'cavalier').
24   *Cobweb :* in fact it was
      Peaseblossom who was ordered to
      scratch.
25   *marvellous :* unusually.
26   *ass :* fool (with obvious irony).

30   *the tongs and the bones :* crude
      musical instruments; tongs were
      struck with a metal key (rather like the
      modern triangle), and bones, were held
      between the fingers and rattled.

32   *peck :* bundle (literally, a quarter
      of a bushel).
      provender : fodder.
34   *bottle :* truss, small bundle.
      fellow : equal.

38   *stir :* disturb.
39   *exposition :* Bottom means
      'disposition' (=desire).
40   *wind :* wrap.
41   *all ways :* in all directions.
42   *woodbine :* bindweed or
      convolvulus.
43   *ivy :* the ivy is said to be female
      because it clings to, and is supported
      by, the elm tree.

Mounsieur, bring me the honey-bag. Do not fret
yourself too much in the action, Mounsieur; and,
15 good Mounsieur, have a care the honey-bag break
not; I would be loath to have you overflown with a
honey-bag, signior. Where's Mounsieur Mustardseed?

Mustardseed
Ready.

Bottom
20 Give me your neaf, Mounsieur Mustardseed. Pray
you, leave your curtsy, good Mounsieur.

Mustardseed
What's your will?

Bottom
Nothing, good Mounsieur, but to help Cavalery
Cobweb to scratch. I must to the barber's,
25 Mounsieur, for methinks I am marvellous hairy
about the face; and I am such a tender ass, if my
hair do but tickle me, I must scratch.

Titania
What, wilt thou hear some music, my sweet love?

Bottom
I have a reasonable good ear in music: let's have the
30 tongs and the bones.

Titania
Or say, sweet love, what thou desir'st to eat.

Bottom
Truly, a peck of provender: I could munch your
good dry oats. Methinks I have a great desire to a
bottle of hay: good hay, sweet hay, hath no fellow.

Titania
35 I have a venturous fairy that shall seek
The squirrel's hoard, and fetch thee new nuts.

Bottom
I had rather have a handful or two of dried peas.
But, I pray you, let none of your people stir me: I
have an exposition of sleep come upon me.

Titania
40 Sleep thou, and I will wind thee in my arms.
Fairies, be gone, and be all ways away.
                              [*Exeunt* Fairies
So doth the woodbine the sweet honeysuckle
Gently entwist; the female ivy so

44 *barky fingers*: branches covered with bark.

Enrings the barky fingers of the elm.
45 O how I love thee! How I dote on thee!

[*They sleep*

Enter Puck

Oberon   [*Coming forward*]
Welcome, good Robin. See'st thou this sweet sight?

47 *dotage*: obsession.
48 *of late*: recently.
49 *favours*: gifts of flowers.
50 *upbraid*: reproach.
51 *rounded*: encircled.

Her dotage now I do begin to pity;
For, meeting her of late behind the wood,
Seeking sweet favours for this hateful fool,
50 I did upbraid her and fall out with her;
For she his hairy temples then had rounded
With coronet of fresh and fragrant flowers;

53 *sometime*: formerly.
54 *orient*: lustrous.
55 *flowerets*: little flowers.

And that same dew, which sometime on the buds
Was wont to swell like round and orient pearls,
55 Stood now within the pretty flowerets' eyes
Like tears that did their own disgrace bewail.
When I had at my pleasure taunted her,

58 *mild terms*: gentle language.
59 *ask of her*: ask her to give me.
60 *straight*: immediately.

And she in mild terms begg'd my patience,
I then did ask of her her changeling child,
60 Which straight she gave me, and her fairy sent
To bear him to my bower in Fairyland.
And now I have the boy, I will undo
This hateful imperfection of her eyes.
And, gentle Puck, take this transformed scalp

66 *other*: others.
67 *repair*: return.
68 *accidents*: happenings.
69 *fierce*: extravagant.

65 From off the head of this Athenian swain,
That he, awaking when the other do,
May all to Athens back again repair,
And think no more of this night's accidents
But as the fierce vexation of a dream.
70 But first I will release the fairy queen.

[*Touching her eyes with a herb*

71 *wont*: accustomed.

Be as thou wast wont to be;
See as thou wast wont to see:
Dian's bud o'er Cupid's flower
Hath such force and blessed power

73 *Dian's bud*: in *Act 2*, scene 1 Oberon explains that he can remove the spell 'with another herb' (line 184). This was perhaps Artemisia, a plant sacred to Diana, goddess of chastity, whose Greek name was Artemis.
    Cupid's flower: see *Act 2*, scene 1 lines 155ff.

75 Now, my Titania, wake you, my sweet queen.
Titania
My Oberon! What visions have I seen!
Methought I was enamour'd of an ass.

77 *enamour'd of*: in love with.
78 *pass*: happen.

Oberon
There lies your love.
Titania   How came these things to pass?

O how mine eyes do loathe his visage now.

Oberon

80 Silence awhile! Robin, take off this head.
Titania, music call; and strike more dead
Than common sleep of all these five the sense.

Titania

Music, ho! Music such as charmeth sleep.

Puck   [*Removing the ass's head from* Bottom]

When thou wak'st, with thine own fool's eyes peep.

Oberon

85 Sound, music! [*Music*] Come, my queen, take
        hands with me,
And rock the ground whereon these sleepers be.
Now thou and I are new in amity,
And will tomorrow midnight solemnly
Dance in Duke Theseus' house triumphantly,
90 And bless it to all fair prosperity.
There shall the pairs of faithful lovers be
Wedded, with Theseus, all in jollity.

Puck

        Fairy king, attend, and mark:
        I do hear the morning lark.

Oberon

95   Then, my queen, in silence sad,
        Trip we after the night's shade;
        We the globe can compass soon,
        Swifter than the wandering moon.

Titania

        Come, my lord; and in our flight
100   Tell me how it came this night
        That I sleeping here was found
        With these mortals on the ground.

                [*Exeunt. Hunting horns sound offstage*

Enter Theseus, Hippolyta, Egeus, *and*
Attendants

Theseus

Go, one of you, find out the forester;
For now our observation is perform'd;
105 And since we have the vaward of the day,
My love shall hear the music of my hounds.
Uncouple in the western valley; let them go.
Dispatch, I say, and find the forester.

81–2   *strike . . . sense :* charm the senses
    of these five people (the four lovers
    and Bottom) to a sleep that is deeper
    than normal sleep.

86   *rock the ground :* i.e. as though the
    ground were a cradle, and the lovers
    were sleeping infants.
87   *amity :* friendship.
88   *solemnly :* ceremoniously.
90   *to :* with.

95   *sad :* sober.

97   *compass :* encompass.

104   *observation :* ritual (to celebrate
    May Day).
105   *since . . . day :* since it is still early
    in the day ('vaward'=earliest part).

107   *uncouple* : unleash; hounds are leashed together in pairs, and trained to keep silent when they are leashed.

108   *Dispatch* : see that it is done quickly.

109   *will* : will go.

110–11   From the top of the mountain they will hear the cry of hounds combined with the echoes.

112–4   Crete and Sparta were both famous, in classical times, for their breed of hounds. Cadmus was founder of Thebes, long before the birth of Hercules, the Greek super-man. No legend tells of the hunting party that Hippolyta refers to.

113   *bay'd* : brought to bay (i.e. drove the bear into a position where it was forced to turn and face the hounds).

115   *chiding* : the noise of angry hounds.

119   *kind* : breed.

120   *flew'd* : with deep, hanging lips and cheeks.
       sanded : with sand-coloured markings.

122   *dew-lapp'd* : with folds of skin (dew-laps) under their chins.
       Thessalian : from Thessaly, a northern part of ancient Greece.

124   *cry* : pack of hounds.

125   *halloo* : the cry made by huntsmen in response to the hounds.
       cheer'd : encouraged.

127   *soft* : wait a minute.
       nymphs : creatures of the woods.

131   *of* : at.

132   *observe* : perform.

133   *our intent* : what we intended to do.

134   *in grace* : to honour.
       solemnity : celebration.

139   *Saint Valentine* : the patron saint of lovers; his feast day (February 14) was traditionally the birds' wedding-day.

140   *to couple* : to form pairs.

[*Exit* Attendant

We will, fair queen, up to the mountain's top,
110 And mark the musical confusion
Of hounds and echo in conjunction.

Hippolyta

I was with Hercules and Cadmus once,
When in a wood of Crete they bay'd the bear
With hounds of Sparta. Never did I hear
115 Such gallant chiding; for besides the groves,
The skies, the fountains, every region near
Seem'd all one mutual cry. I never heard
So musical a discord, such sweet thunder.

Theseus

My hounds are bred out of the Spartan kind:
120 So flew'd, so sanded; and their heads are hung
With ears that sweep away the morning dew;
Crook-knee'd, and dew-lapp'd like Thessalian
     bulls;
Slow in pursuit, but match'd in mouth like bells,
Each under each. A cry more tuneable
125 Was never halloo'd to, nor cheer'd with horn,
In Crete, in Sparta, nor in Thessaly.
Judge, when you hear. But soft, what nymphs are
     these?

Egeus

My lord, this is my daughter here asleep;
And this, Lysander; this Demetrius is;
130 This Helena, old Nedar's Helena:
I wonder of their being here together.

Theseus

No doubt they rose up early to observe
The rite of May; and, hearing our intent,
Came here in grace of our solemnity.
135 But speak, Egeus, is not this the day
That Hermia should give answer of her choice?

Egeus

It is, my lord.

Theseus

Go, bid the huntsmen wake them with their horns.
[*Horns and shouts offstage. The lovers wake and jump
                                          to their feet*
Good morrow, friends. Saint Valentine is past:
140 Begin these wood-birds but to couple now?

Lysander
Pardon, my lord.   [*The lovers kneel*
  Theseus   I pray you all, stand up.
I know you two are rival enemies:
How comes this gentle concord in the world,
That hatred is so far from jealousy,
145 To sleep by hate, and fear no enmity?
  Lysander
My lord, I shall reply amazedly,
Half sleep, half waking: but as yet, I swear,
I cannot truly say how I came here;
But, as I think—for truly would I speak,
150 And now I do bethink me, so it is—
I came with Hermia hither: our intent
Was to be gone from Athens, where we might,
Without the peril of the Athenian law—
  Egeus
Enough, enough, my lord; you have enough!
155 I beg the law, the law upon his head.
They would have stol'n away; they would, De-
  metrius,
Thereby to have defeated you and me—
You of your wife, and me of my consent—
Of my consent that she should be your wife.
  Demetrius
160 My lord, fair Helen told me of their stealth,
Of this their purpose hither to this wood;
And I in fury hither follow'd them,
Fair Helena in fancy following me.
But, my good lord, I wot not by what power—
165 But by some power it is—my love to Hermia,
Melted as the snow, seems to me now
As the remembrance of an idle gaud
Which in my childhood I did dote upon;
And all the faith, the virtue of my heart,
170 The object and the pleasure of mine eye,
Is only Helena. To her, my lord,
Was I betroth'd ere I saw Hermia;
But, like a sickness, did I loathe this food.
But, as in health, come to my natural taste,
175 Now do I wish it, love it, long for it,
And will for evermore be true to it.

142   *rival enemies :* enemies in rivalry
     (for Hermia's love).
144   *jealousy :* suspicion.
145   *by hate :* by the side of one who
     hates you.

146   *amazedly :* in confusion.

153   *Without :* out of reach of.

157   *defeated :* deprived.

160   *stealth :* secret escape.
161   *purpose hither :* intention to come
     here.

163   *in fancy :* in her love.
164   *wot :* know.

167   *idle :* useless.
     gaud : toy.

169   *virtue :* power.

172   *ere :* before.
173   *like sickness :* like a sick man.
174   *come :* returned.

Theseus
Fair lovers, you are fortunately met:
Of this discourse we more will hear anon.
Egeus, I will overbear your will,
180 For in the temple by and by with us,
These couples shall eternally be knit.
And—for the morning now is something worn—
Our purpos'd hunting shall be set aside.
Away with us to Athens. Three and three,
185 We'll hold a feast in great solemnity.
Come, Hippolyta.

[*Exeunt* Theseus, Hippolyta, Egeus, *and*
Attendants

Demetrius
These things seem small and undistinguishable,
Like far-off mountains turned into clouds.
Hermia
Methinks I see these things with parted eye,
190 When everything seems double.   **Helena**   So methinks:
And I have found Demetrius, like a jewel,
Mine own, and not mine own.   **Demetrius**   Are you sure
That we are awake? It seems to me
That yet we sleep, we dream. Do not you think
195 The duke was here, and bid us follow him?
Hermia
Yea, and my father.
Helena   And Hippolyta.
Lysander
And he did bid us follow to the temple.
Demetrius
Why then, we are awake. Let's follow him,
And by the way let us recount our dreams. [*Exeunt*
Bottom   [*Waking*]
200 When my cue comes, call me, and I will
answer: my next is, 'Most fair Pyramus'.
Heigh-ho! Peter Quince! Flute, the bellows-
mender! Snout, the tinker! Starveling! God's my
life—stolen hence and left me asleep! I have had a
205 most rare vision. I have had a dream—past the wit
of man to say what dream it was: man is but an ass,

178 *anon :* presently.
179 *overbear :* over-rule.

182 *something worn :* almost gone.
183 *purpos'd :* intended.
184 *Three and three :* three men and three women.
185 *solemnity :* splendour.
     parted eye : double vision

189 *parted eye :* double vision
     (where the eyes do not focus together).

199 *cue :* Bottom thinks he is still at the rehearsal.

200 *next :* i.e. next cue.

206   *go about* : try.
       expound : explain.
209   *patched fool* : professional jesters
       wore multi-coloured suits which might
       look as though they had been
       'patched'.
210–14 *The eye . . . dream was* : Bottom's
       phrasing is influenced by his confused
       memory of the first Epistle to the
       Corinthians, 2:9.
213   *ballad* : the sixteenth-century
       equivalent of a newspaper: ballads
       telling of strange events were sung to
       popular tunes.
215   *no bottom* : no foundation in
       reality.
216   *peradventure* : perhaps.
217   *gracious* : pleasing.
       her : i.e. Thisbe's.

if he go about to expound this dream. Methought I
was—there is no man can tell what. Methought I
was—and methought I had—but man is but a
210 patched fool if he will offer to say what methought I
had. The eye of man hath not heard, the ear of man
hath not seen, man's hand is not able to taste, his
tongue to conceive, nor his heart to report, what my
dream was. I will get Peter Quince to write a ballad
215 of this dream: it shall be called 'Bottom's Dream',
because it hath no bottom; and I will sing it in the
latter end of a play before the duke: peradventure,
to make it the more gracious, I shall sing it at her
death.   [*Exit*

Act 4   Scene 2
The Athenian workmen are lamenting
the loss of Bottom when suddenly he
appears, with goods news about their
play.

3   *Out of doubt* : without doubt,
       certainly.

4   *transported* : carried away (by
       spirits).

5   *marred* : spoiled.
5–6   *it . . . forward* : we do not go on
       with it.

8   *discharge* : play the part of.

9   *wit* : brain.
       handicraft man : tradesman.

11   *person* : appearance.
12   *paramour* : unlawful lover.

13   *paragon* : model of excellence.
14   *thing of naught* : wicked thing.

Scene 2 *Athens : a room in* Quince's *house*

Enter Quince, Flute, Snout *and* Starveling

Quince
Have you sent to Bottom's house? Is he come home
yet?
Starveling
He cannot be heard of. Out of doubt he is
transported.
Flute
5 If he come not, then the play is marred: it goes not
forward, doth it?
Quince
It is not possible: you have not a man in all Athens
able to discharge Pyramus but he.
Flute
No, he hath simply the best wit of any handicraft
10 man in Athens.
Quince
Yea, and the best person too; and he is a very
paramour for a sweet voice.
Flute
You must say, 'paragon': a paramour is—God
bless us—a thing of naught.

17   *gone forward* : taken place.
     made men : men who had made
     their fortunes.
19   *bully* : good fellow.

19–20   *sixpence . . . life* : a nobleman
        (such as Theseus) might reward
        faithful servants by giving them a
        regular pension for the rest of
        ('during') their lives. At the time
        Shakespeare wrote this play, a day's
        wages for a tradesman was about
        fourpence.
20   *'scaped* : missed.
21   *An* : if.
25   *hearts* : good fellows.
26   *courageous* : Quince perhaps
     means 'auspicious' (=favourable).
     happy : lucky.
28   *I am* : I have to.

30   *right . . . out* : exactly as it
     happened.

32   *of me* : about me:
33   *apparel* : costumes.
34   *strings* : i.e. to tie the false beards
     on.
     pumps : dancing-shoes.
35   *presently* : immediately.
37   *preferred* : put on the list of
     possible entertainments.
     In any case : whatever happens.
38   *pare* : clip.

41   *sweet breath* : sweet words (which
     must not be spoiled by bad breath).

Enter Snug

Snug

15 Masters, the duke is coming from the temple, and
    there is two or three lords and ladies more married:
    if our sport had gone forward, we had all been made
    men.

Flute

O sweet bully Bottom! Thus hath he lost sixpence a
20 day during his life; he could not have 'scaped
    sixpence a day. An the duke had not given him
    sixpence a day for playing Pyramus, I'll be hanged;
    he would have deserved it. Sixpence a day in
    Pyramus, or nothing.

Enter Bottom

Bottom

25 Where are these lads? Where are these hearts?

Quince

Bottom! O most courageous day! O most happy
hour!

Bottom

Masters, I am to discourse wonders—but ask me
not what; for if I tell you, I am not true Athenian. I
30 will tell you everything, right as it fell out.

Quince

Let us hear, sweet Bottom.

Bottom

Not a word of me. All that I will tell you is, that the
duke hath dined. Get your apparel together, good
strings to your beards, new ribbons to your pumps.
35 Meet presently at the palace. Every man look o'er
    his part, for the short and the long is, our play is
    preferred. In any case, let Thisbe have clean linen;
    and let not him that plays the lion pare his nails, for
    they shall hang out for the lion's claws. And, most
40 dear actors, eat no onions nor garlic, for we are to
    utter sweet breath, and I do not doubt but to hear
    them say it is a sweet comedy. No more words:
    away! Go—away.   [*Exeunt*

Act 5

Act 5   Scene 1
After their marriage Theseus and
Hippolyta, with the other four lovers,
watch the performance of 'Pyramus
and Thisbe'. They are all greatly
amused. When the play is finished,
and everyone has gone to bed, the
fairies return to bless the married
couples.

3   *antique* : ancient.
       toys : tales.
4   *seething* : boiling, over-active.
5   *shaping fantasies* : inventive
imaginations.
       apprehend : conceive.
6   *comprehends* : understands.
7   *compact* : composed.

11   *Helen* : Helen of Troy, the most
beautiful woman in the world
(according to classical authors).
       a brow of Egypt : the face of a
gipsy.
14   *bodies forth* : expresses.

Scene 1 *Athens : the palace of Theseus*

Enter Theseus, Hippolyta, Philostrate,
and Attendants

Hippolyta
'Tis strange, my Theseus, that these lovers speak
  of.
  Theseus
More strange than true. I never may believe
These antique fables, nor these fairy toys.
Lovers and madmen have such seething brains,
5 Such shaping fantasies, that apprehend
More than cool reason ever comprehends.
The lunatic, the lover, and the poet,
Are of imagination all compact.
One sees more devils than vast hell can hold :
10 That is the madman ; the lover, all as frantic,
Sees Helen's beauty in a brow of Egypt ;
The poet's eye, in a fine frenzy rolling,
Doth glance from heaven to earth, from earth to
heaven ;
And, as imagination bodies forth
15 The forms of things unknown, the poet's pen

kinsman : Theseus and Hercules, [c]lassical super-man, were cousins.	We'll none of that: that have I told my love,
tipsy : drunken.	In glory of my kinsman Hercules.
	The riot of the tipsy Bacchanals,
	Tearing the Thracian singer in their rage.
device : theatrical production.	50 That is an old device, and it was play'd
came last : the last time that I	When I from Thebes came last a conqueror.
	The thrice three Muses mourning for the death
thrice three Muses : in classical [myth]ology there are nine Muses.	*Of learning, late deceas'd in beggary.*
late : recently.	That is some satire, keen and critical,
beggary : poverty.	55 Not sorting with a nuptial ceremony.
keen : biting.	*A tedious brief scene of young Pyramus*
sorting with : appropriate to.	*And his love Thisbe ; very tragical mirth.*
	Merry and tragical? Tedious and brief?
	That is, hot ice and wondrous strange snow.
concord : harmony.	60 How shall we find the concord of this discord?
	Philostrate
	A play there is, my lord, some ten words long,
	Which is as brief as I have known a play;
	But by ten words, my lord, it is too long,
	Which makes it tedious; for in all the play
fitted : suited to his role.	65 There is not one word apt, one player fitted.
	And tragical, my noble lord, it is,
	For Pyramus therein doth kill himself—
	Which when I saw rehears'd, I must confess,
	Made mine eyes water; but more merry tears
	70 The passion of loud laughter never shed.
	Theseus
	What are they that do play it?
	Philostrate
Hard-handed men : labourers (not [gen]tlemen).	Hard-handed men that work in Athens here,
labour'd in their minds : engaged in [inte]llectual exercise.	Which never labour'd in their minds till now,
	And now have toil'd their unbreath'd memories
unbreath'd : untrained.	75 With this same play, against your nuptial.
against : in preparation for.	**Theseus**
	And we will hear it.
for you : suitable for you.	**Philostrate** No, my noble lord;
over : through.	It is not for you; I have heard it over,
sport : amusement.	And it is nothing, nothing in the world;
intent : intentions.	Unless you can find sport in their intents,
stretch'd : put to great effort.	80 Extremely stretch'd and conn'd with cruel pain,
conn'd : learned by heart.	To do you service.
do you service : be of service to	**Theseus** I will hear that play;
amiss : wrong.	For never anything can be amiss

17   *local habitation :* particular
dwelling-place.
       name : identity.
19   *apprehend :* conceive.
20   *comprehends :* includes in its
conception.

23–6   But the story of the night, and the
way that their minds were all affected
('transfigur'd') in the same way, at the
same time, is evidence that there is
more to the affair than fanciful
invention; it adds up to ('grows to')
something very consistent ('constant').
27   *howsoever :* anyway.
       admirable : to be marvelled at.

30   *More :* i.e. more joy.

31   *walks :* wherever you go.
       board : table.
32   *masques :* entertainments with
music and dancing.
33   *wear :* pass.
34   *after-supper :* light meal of fruit
and sweets, served after the main meal.
35   *manager of mirth :* entertainments
organiser.
36   *revels :* amusements.
       in hand : available.

39   *abridgement :* pastime.
40   *beguile :* spend.

42   *brief :* programme.
       sports : entertainments.
       ripe : ready.

44–45 See p. iv.

Turns them to shapes, and gi
A local habitation and a name   47
Such tricks hath strong imagi   the
That if it would but apprehen   48
20 It comprehends some bringer   50
Or in the night, imagining som   51
How easy is a bush suppos'd a   52   cam
       Hippolyta   myt
But all the story of the night to   53
And all their minds transfigur'd
25 More witnesseth than fancy's in   54
And grows to something of grea   55
But, howsoever, strange and adm

       Enter Lysander, Der   60
       and Helena
       Theseus
Here come the lovers, full of joy
Joy, gentle friends, joy and fresh
30 Accompany your hearts!
       Lysander   65
Wait in your royal walks, your bo
       Theseus
Come now, what masques, what
       have
To wear away this long age of thr
Between our after-supper and be
35 Where is our usual manager of m
What revels are in hand? Is there
To ease the anguish of a torturin   72
Call Philostrate.   ge
       Philostrate   Here   73
       Theseus   in
Say, what abridgement have you   74
40 What masque, what music? How   75
The lazy time if not with some   77
       Philostrate
There is a brief how many spor   79
Make choice of which your high
                                               80

       Theseus   81
The battle with the Centaurs, to   yo
45 *By an Athenian eunuch to the h*   82

83 *simpleness :* innocence.
   tender : offer.

85 *wretchedness :* weakness, disability.
   o'ercharg'd : overburdened.
86 *duty . . . perishing :* people who are
   trying to do their duty but who fail in
   their efforts to please.

88 *they . . . kind :* they have no skill
   in this sort of thing.

90 *take :* take in good part, accept
   graciously.
91 *respect :* consideration.
92 Takes the will for the deed—i.e.
   judges by the intention, not the
   accomplishment.
93 *Where . . . come :* in some places
   that I have visited.
   clerks : scholars.
94 *premeditated welcomes :* carefully
   prepared speeches of welcome.
96 *periods :* pauses.
97 *Throttle :* choke.
   practis'd accents : carefully
   rehearsed speeches.
   fears : nervousness.
101 *modesty :* embarrassment.
   fearful duty : nervousness caused
   by their sense of duty.
102 *rattling :* chattering.
104 *tongue-tied :* speechless.
105 *In least :* in few words.
   capacity : understanding.
106 *address'd :* ready to begin.

108–17 Quince is nervous, and he makes
   nonsense of the Prologue in exactly the
   way described by Theseus in line 96.
108 *will :* intention.
112 *but in despite :* only to annoy you.

When simpleness and duty tender it.
Go, bring them in: and take your places, ladies.
                              [*Exit* Philostrate

Hippolyta
85 I love not to see wretchedness o'ercharg'd,
   And duty in his service perishing.
Theseus
   Why, gentle sweet, you shall see no such thing.
Hippolyta
   He says they can do nothing in this kind.
Theseus
   The kinder we, to give them thanks for nothing.
90 Our sport shall be to take what they mistake:
   And what poor duty cannot do, noble respect
   Takes it in might, not merit.
   Where I have come, great clerks have purposed
   To greet me with premeditated welcomes;
95 Where I have seen them shiver and look pale,
   Make periods in the midst of sentences,
   Throttle their practis'd accents in their fears,
   And, in conclusion, dumbly have broke off,
   Not paying me a welcome. Trust me, sweet,
100 Out of this silence yet I pick'd a welcome;
   And in the modesty of fearful duty
   I read as much as from the rattling tongue
   Of saucy and audacious eloquence.
   Love, therefore, and tongue-tied simplicity
105 In least speak most, to my capacity.

          Enter Philostrate

Philostrate
So please your grace, the Prologue is address'd.
Theseus
Let him approach.

          [*Flourish of trumpets*

          Enter Quince *as the* Prologue.
Quince
If we offend, it is with our good will.
   That you should think we come not to offend
110 But with good will. To show our simple skill,
   That is the true beginning of our end.
   Consider then we come but in despite.

113   *minding* : meaning.

We do not come as minding to content you,
Our true intent is. All for your delight,
115   We are not here. That you should here repent you,
The actors are at hand; and by their show,
You shall know all that you are like to know.

116   *at hand* : ready.
show : performance.

Theseus

This fellow doth not stand upon points.

118   *stand upon* : pay attention to.
points : punctuation.

Lysander

119   *rid* : ridden.
rough : unbroken.

He hath rid his prologue like a rough colt; he knows
120 not the stop. A good moral, my lord: it is not
enough to speak, but to speak true.

120   *the stop* : when to stop (either at
the full stop in reading, or when a
horse is reined in).
121   *true* : properly.
123   *government* : control.

Hippolyta

Indeed he hath played on his prologue like a child
on a recorder—a sound, but not in government.

Theseus

His speech was like a tangled chain: nothing
125 impaired, but all disordered. Who is next?

Enter a Trumpeter, *followed by* Bottom
as Pyramus, Flute *as Thisbe,* Snout *as
Wall,* Starveling *as Moonshine, and* Snug
as Lion.

Quince

126   *Gentles* : the normal address,
equivalent to the modern 'Ladies and
Gentlemen'.
perchance : perhaps.

Gentles, perchance you wonder at this show;
But wonder on, till truth make all things plain.
This man is Pyramus, if you would know;
This beauteous lady Thisbe is, certain.
130   This man, with lime and rough-cast, doth
present
Wall, that vile Wall which did these lovers
sunder;
And through Wall's chink, poor souls, they are
content
To whisper. At the which let no man wonder.
This man, with lantern, dog, and bush of thorn,

134   See note to *3,1.58*.

135   Presenteth Moonshine; for, if you will know,
By moonshine did these lovers think no scorn
To meet at Ninus' tomb, there, there to woo.
This grisly beast, which Lion hight by name,

138   *hight* : is called.

The trusty Thisbe, coming first by night,
140   Did scare away, or rather did affright;

141   *fall* : drop.

And, as she fled, her mantle she did fall,

143 *Anon :* presently.
   tall : brave.

145 *Whereat :* whereupon.
   blade : sword.

146 *broach'd :* pierced.

147 *tarrying :* waiting.

149 *twain :* both.

150 *At large :* at full length.

151 *be to speak :* is going to speak.

154 *interlude :* short play.
   befall : happen.

155 *present :* represent.

157 *crannied :* cracked.

162 *right and sinister :* to the right and
   to the left.

164 *lime and hair :* from which bricks
   were made.

165 *wittiest :* most intelligent.
   partition : Demetrius plays with
   two meanings of the word—(a)
   dividing wall; and (b) section of a
   speech or composition.

Which Lion vile with bloody mouth did stain.
Anon comes Pyramus, sweet youth and tall,
 And finds his trusty Thisbe's mantle slain :
145 Whereat with blade, with bloody blameful blade,
 He bravely broach'd his boiling bloody breast;
And Thisbe, tarrying in mulberry shade,
 His dagger drew, and died. For all the rest,
Let Lion, Moonshine, Wall, and lovers twain,
150 At large discourse, while here they do remain.

         [*Exeunt* Quince, Bottom, Flute, Snug *and*
                                    Starveling

Theseus
I wonder if the lion be to speak.

Demetrius
No wonder, my lord : one lion may, when many
asses do.

Snout
In this same interlude it doth befall
155 That I, one Snout by name, present a wall;
And such a wall, as I would have you think,
That had in it a crannied hole or chink,
Through which the lovers, Pyramus and Thisbe,
Did whisper often, very secretly.
160 This loam, this roughcast, and this stone doth
show
That I am that same wall; the truth is so.
And this the cranny is, right and sinister,
Through which the fearful lovers are to whisper.

Theseus
Would you desire lime and hair to speak better?

Demetrius
165 It is the wittiest partition that ever I heard
discourse, my lord.

Theseus
Pyramus draws near the wall : silence!

         Enter Bottom

Bottom
O grim-look'd night! O night with hue so black!
 O night, which ever art when day is not!
170 O night! O night! Alack, alack, alack!
 I fear my Thisbe's promise is forgot.
And thou, O wall! O sweet, O lovely wall!

That stand'st between her father's ground
 and mine;
Thou wall, O wall! O sweet, and lovely wall,

175 Show me thy chink to blink through with mine
 eyne.
       [Snout *holds up his fingers.*
Thanks, courteous wall: Jove shield thee well for
 this!
 But what see I? No Thisbe do I see.
O wicked wall, through whom I see no bliss;
 Curs'd be thy stones for thus deceiving me!

Theseus

180 The wall, methinks, being sensible, should curse
 again.

Bottom

No, in truth, sir, he should not. 'Deceiving me' is
Thisbe's cue: she is to enter now, and I am to spy
her through the wall. You shall see, it will fall pat as
185 I told you. Yonder she comes.

    Enter Flute

Flute

O wall, full often hast thou heard my moans,
 For parting my fair Pyramus and me:
My cherry lips have often kiss'd thy stones,
 Thy stones with lime and hair knit up in thee.

Bottom

190 I see a voice: now will I to the chink,
 To spy an I can hear my Thisbe's face.
Thisbe!

Flute

    My love! Thou art my love, I think.

Bottom

Think what thou wilt, I am thy lover's grace;
And, like Limander, am I trusty still.

Flute

195 And I like Helen, till the Fates me kill.

Bottom

Not Shafalus to Procrus was so true.

Flute

As Shafalus to Procrus, I to you.

Bottom

O, kiss me through the hole of this vile wall.

175 *eyne :* eyes.

180 *sensible :* capable of feeling.

181 *again :* in reply.

184 *fall :* happen.
   pat : exactly.

191 *an :* if.

193 *lover's grace :* gracious lover.
194–6 *Limander :* Bottom intends to
 refer to Leander, a classical lover who
 was drowned when swimming to reach
 his love, Hero, whom Flute miscalls
 'Helen'. Helen's lover was the Trojan
 Paris. Cephalus (whose name is also
 mispronounced by Bottom) was
 renowed in classical mythology for
 faithfulness to his wife Procris.
195 *the Fates :* the three sisters who, in
 classical mythology, ruled over the
 lives of men.

Flute
I kiss the wall's hole, not your lips at all.

Bottom
200 Wilt thou at Ninny's tomb meet me straightway?

Flute
'Tide life, 'tide death, I come without delay.

[*Exeunt* Bottom *and* Flute

Snout
Thus have I, Wall, my part discharged so;
And being done, thus Wall away doth go.

[*Exit*

Theseus
Now is the mural down between the two neigh-
205 bours.

Demetrius
No remedy, my lord, when walls are so wilful to
hear without warning.

Hippolyta
This is the silliest stuff that ever I heard.

Theseus
The best in this kind are but shadows, and the
210 worst are no worse, if imagination amend them.

Hippolyta
It must be your imagination then, and not theirs.

Theseus
If we imagine no worse of them than they of
themselves, they may pass for excellent men. Here
come two noble beasts in, a man and a lion.

Enter Snug *and* Starveling

Snug
215 You, ladies, you whose gentle hearts do fear
    The smallest monstrous mouse that creeps on
        floor,
    May now perchance both quake and tremble
        here.
    When lion rough in wildest rage doth roar.
Then know that I one Snug the joiner am
220 A lion fell, nor else no lion's dam:
For if I should as lion come in strife
Into this place, 'twere pity on my life.

Theseus
A very gentle beast, and of a good conscience.

---

200 *Ninny* : see note to 3,1.95.
     straightway : immediately.

201 *'Tide* : betide, come.

202 *discharged* : performed.

204 *mural* : wall.

206 *No remedy* : there is no help for
     it.
     to : as to.

209 *The best . . . kind* : the best actors.
     but : only.
210 *amend them* : make up for their
     deficiencies.

213 *pass for* : be counted as.
214 *in* : on to the stage.

220 *fell* : savage.
     dam : mother.
222 *'twere . . . life* : I would have to
     ask you to have pity on my life
     (because he would have deserved
     punishment).
223 *gentle* : polite.

Demetrius

The very best at a beast, my lord, that e'er I saw.

Lysander

225 This lion is a very fox for his valour.

Theseus

True; and a goose for his discretion.

Demetrius

Not so, my lord; for his valour cannot carry his discretion, and the fox carries the goose.

Theseus

His discretion, I am sure, cannot carry his valour,
230 for the goose carries not the fox. It is well: leave it to his discretion, and let us listen to the moon.

Starveling

This lantern doth the horned moon present—

Demetrius

He should have worn the horns on his head.

Theseus

He is no crescent, and his horns are invisible within
235 the circumference.

Starveling

This lantern doth the horned moon present;
Myself the man i' the moon do seem to be.

Theseus

This is the greatest error of all the rest. The man should be put into the lantern: how is it else the
240 man i' the moon?

Demetrius

He dares not come there for the candle; for, you see, it is already in snuff.

225   *very :* real.
    fox : the fox is cunning rather than brave.

227   *cannot carry :* cannot conquer.
228   *carries :* carries off.

232   *horned moon :* crescent moon.
233   *He . . . head :* men with unfaithful wives were said to have horns on their heads.
234–5 When the moon is full we do not see the 'horns' because they have grown into the full circle ('circumference').
237   *man i' the moon :* see note to *3*,1.58.
242   *in snuff :* the candle needs to be snuffed out (=have the burnt part of the wick removed); and 'in snuff' also meant 'in a bad temper'.

THE HORNED MOON

Hippolyta

I am aweary of this moon: would he would change!

Theseus

It appears, by his small light of discretion, that he is
in the wane; but yet, in courtesy, in all reason, we
must stay the time.

Lysander

Proceed, Moon.

Starveling

All that I have to say is to tell you that the lantern is
the moon; I, the man in the moon; this thorn-bush,
my thorn-bush; and this dog, my dog.

Demetrius

Why, all these should be in the lantern; for all these
are in the moon. But silence—here comes Thisbe.

Enter Flute

Flute

This is old Ninny's tomb. Where is my love?

Snug

[*Roaring*] Oh—.   [Flute *runs off*

Demetrius

Well roared, Lion!

Theseus

Well, run, Thisbe!

Hippolyta

Well shone, Moon! Truly, the moon shines with a
good grace.
                   [*The* Lion *tears* Thisbe's *mantle; exit*

Theseus

Well moused, Lion!

Demetrius

And then came Pyramus.

Lysander

And so the lion vanished.

Enter Bottom

Bottom

Sweet moon, I thank thee for thy sunny beams;
   I thank thee, moon, for shining now so bright,
For, by thy gracious, golden, glittering gleams,
   I trust to taste of truest Thisbe's sight.
      But stay, O spite!

245   *in courtesy*: it is polite.
      in all reason: it is only reasonable.
246   *stay the time*: wait for the right
      time.

259   *moused*: perhaps the Lion looked
      more like a cat shaking a mouse.

266   *spite*: disaster.

268 *dole* : cause for grief.

274 *Furies* : the creatures in Greek mythology who pursued those guilty of murder.

275 *Fates* : the three sisters in classical mythology who ruled over the life of man; they were pictured weaving the thread of life, measuring it out, and finally cutting it when the man was to die.

276 *thread and thrum* : everything; the 'thrum' is a special thread used in weaving.

277 *Quail* : overpower.
     quell : slay.

280 *Beshrew* : curse.

281 *frame* : construct.

282 *deflower'd* : ravished, carried off.

284 *look'd with cheer* : looked with her face.

285 *confound* : destroy.

287 *pap* : breast.

297 *die* : one of a pair of dice.
     ace : the single spot on a dice.

But mark, poor knight,
What dreadful dole is here?
Eyes, do you see?
270   How can it be?
O dainty duck! O dear!
Thy mantle good,
What, stain'd with blood!
Approach, ye Furies fell!
275   O Fates, come, come,
Cut thread and thrum;
Quail, crush, conclude, and quell!

Theseus
This passion, and the death of a dear friend, would
go near to make a man look sad.

Hippolyta
280 Beshrew my heart, but I pity the man.

Bottom
O wherefore, Nature, didst thou lions frame,
Since lion vile hath here deflower'd my dear?
Which is—no, no—which was the fairest dame
That liv'd, that lov'd, that lik'd, that look'd with
     cheer.
285   Come tears, confound;
Out, sword and wound
The pap of Pyramus:
Ay, that left pap,
Where heart doth hop:
290   Thus die I, thus, thus, thus.
                              [*Stabs himself*
Now am I dead,
Now am I fled;
My soul is in the sky:
Tongue, lose thy light!
295   Moon, take thy flight!
                              [*Exit* Starveling
Now die, die, die, die, die.   [*Dies*

Demetrius
No die, but an ace for him; for he is but one.

Lysander
Less than an ace, man, for he is dead; he is nothing.

Theseus
With the help of a surgeon he might yet recover,
300 and prove an ass.

Hippolyta

How chance Moonshine is gone before Thisbe comes back and finds her lover?

Theseus

She will find him by starlight. Here she comes; and her passion ends the play.

Enter Flute

Hippolyta

305 Methinks she should not use a long one for such a Pyramus: I hope she will be brief.

Demetrius

A mote will turn the balance, which Pyramus, which Thisbe, is the better: he for a man, God warrant us; she for a woman, God bless us.

Lysander

310 She hath spied him already with those sweet eyes.

Demetrius

And thus she means, *videlicet*:—

Flute

Asleep, my love?
What dead, my dove?
O Pyramus, arise!
315   Speak, speak! Quite dumb?
Dead, dead! A tomb
Must cover thy sweet eyes.
These lily lips,
This cherry nose,
320   These yellow cowslip cheeks,
Are gone, are gone:
Lovers, make moan!
His eyes were green as leeks.
O Sisters Three,
325   Come, come to me,
With hands as pale as milk;
Lay them in gore,
Since you have shore
With shears his thread of silk.
330   Tongue, not a word!
Come, trusty sword:
Come, blade, my breast imbrue:
And farewell, friends;   [*Stabs herself*
Thus Thisbe ends:

---

301   *How chance :* how does it happen that?

307   *mote :* speck of dust.
307–8   *which Pyramus, which Thisbe :* whether Pyramus or Thisbe.
309   *warrant :* defend.

310   *spied :* caught sight of.

311   *means :* moans.
        videlicet : namely.

314   *Sisters Three :* see note to line 275.

327   *gore :* blood.
328   *shore :* shorn.

332   *imbrue :* pierce.

336   *left :* left alive.

335   Adieu, adieu, adieu.   [*Dies*

Theseus

Moonshine and Lion are left to bury the dead.

Demetrius

Ay, and Wall too.

Bottom

No, I assure you; the wall is down that parted their
fathers. Will it please you to see the epilogue, or to

340   *Bergomask dance :* country dance
originating in Bergamo (Italy).

340 hear a Bergomask dance between two of our
company?

Theseus

342–3   *No . . . excuse.* In the epilogue, it
was quite usual for the writer to ask
the audience to excuse the play's
failings (as Puck does at the end of *A
Midsummer Night's Dream*).

344   *Marry :* by the Virgin Mary.
345   *writ :* wrote.
347   *notably :* commendably.
348   *discharged :* performed.
348–9   *let . . . alone :* forget about the
epilogue.
350   *told :* counted, struck.
351   *fairy time :* i.e. from midnight to
dawn.
352   *out-sleep :* sleep late.
353   *overwatch'd :* stayed up late.
354   *palpable-gross :* dreadfully crude.
354–5   *beguil'd . . . night :* amused us so
that we did not feel that time was
passing slowly tonight.
356   *solemnity :* celebration.
357   *In nightly revels :* with
entertainments every night.
358   *behowls :* howls at.

No epilogue, I pray you; for your play needs no
excuse. Never excuse; for when the players are all
dead, there need none to be blamed. Marry, if he

345 that writ it had played Pyramus, and hanged
himself in Thisbe's garter, it would have been a fine
tragedy: and so it is, truly, and very notably
discharged. But come, your Bergomask: let your
epilogue alone.

       [Bottom *and his friends dance, then exeunt*

350 The iron tongue of midnight hath told twelve;
Lovers, to bed; 'tis almost fairy time.
I fear we shall out-sleep the coming morn,
As much as we this night have overwatch'd.
This palpable-gross play hath well beguil'd

355 The heavy gait of night. Sweet friends, to bed.
A fortnight hold we this solemnity,
In nightly revels, and new jollity.   [*Exeunt*

Enter Puck

Puck

Now the hungry lion roars,
    And the wolf behowls the moon;

360   *heavy :* exhausted.
361   *fordone :* tired out.
362   *wasted :* burnt-out.
       brands : logs of wood (on the fire).
363   *screech-owl :* the Elizabethans
thought that this bird's cry was
ominous, foretelling death.
365   *shroud :* i.e. of death.

360 Whilst the heavy ploughman snores,
    All with weary task fordone.
Now the wasted brands do glow,
    Whilst the screech-owl, screeching loud,
Puts the wretch that lies in woe

365   In remembrance of a shroud.
Now it is the time of night
    That the graves, all gaping wide,
Every one lets forth his sprite,
    In the church-way paths to glide:

368   *his sprite :* the ghost of the man
buried there.

371   *triple Hecate :* Hecate (here pronounced with only two syllables) was goddess of darkness and magic; she had three identities—as Luna in heaven, Diana on earth, and Hecate in the underworld.

373   *frolic :* playful.

376–7   Robin Goodfellow was traditionally represented with a broom because it was his job to keep the house clean.

377   *behind :* from behind (where the human servants had failed to clean).

378   *glimmering :* flickering.

380   *sprite :* spirit.

382   *ditty :* song.

384   *rehearse . . . rote :* repeat your song from memory.

390   *best bride-bed :* i.e. that of Theseus and Hippolyta.

392   *issue :* children.
        create : conceived.
393   *fortunate :* lucky.

396   *blots :* mistakes.
397   *stand :* be seen.
398   *mark prodigious :* ominous birthmark (thought to foretell bad luck for the child).

402   *consecrate :* consecrated.
403   *take his gait :* make his way.
404   *several :* separate.

370   And we fairies, that do run
            By the triple Hecate's team,
        From the presence of the sun,
            Following darkness like a dream,
        Now are frolic; not a mouse
375   Shall disturb this hallow'd house:
        I am sent with broom before,
        To sweep the dust behind the door.

Enter Oberon *and* Titania, *with their* Attendants

Oberon
Through the house give glimmering light
By the dead and drowsy fire;
380 Every elf and fairy sprite
Hop as light as bird from brier;
And this ditty after me
Sing and dance it trippingly.

Titania
First, rehearse your song by rote,
385 To each word a warbling note:
Hand in hand, with fairy grace,
Will we sing, and bless this place.

[*Song and dance*

Now, until the break of day,
Through this house each fairy stray.
390 To the best bride-bed will we,
Which by us shall blessed be;
And the issue there create
Ever shall be fortunate.
So shall all the couples three
395 Ever true in loving be;
And the blots of Nature's hand
Shall not in their issue stand:
Never mole, hare-lip, nor scar,
Nor mark prodigious, such as are
400 Despised in nativity,
Shall upon their children be.
With this field-dew consecrate,
Every fairy take his gait,
And each several chamber bless,
405 Through this palace, with sweet peace;
And the owner of it blest,

Ever shall in safety rest.
    Trip away;
    Make no stay;
410 Meet me all by break of day.
            [*Exeunt* Oberon, Titania, *and* Attendants
         Puck
411   *shadows :* (a) fairies; and (b)   If we shadows have offended,
       actors.   Think but this, and all is mended:
                                            That you have but slumber'd here
                                            While these visions did appear.
415   *idle :* foolish.   415 And this weak and idle theme,
416   *no more yielding :* offering no more   No more yielding but a dream,
       than.   Gentles, do not reprehend:
417   *Gentles :* ladies and gentlemen.   If you pardon, we will mend.
       reprehend : blame.   And, as I am an honest Puck,
418   *mend :* improve.   420 If we have unearned luck
420   *unearned :* undeserved.   Now to 'scape the serpent's tongue,
421   *'scape :* escape.   We will make amends ere long;
       the serpent's tongue : the hissing   Else the puck a liar call:
       that indicates an audience's   So, good night unto you all.
       disapproval.   425 Give me your hands, if we be friends,
422   *make amends :* repay you.   And Robin shall restore amends.   [*Exit*
       ere : before.
423   *puck :* see p. ix.
425   *give me your hands :* i.e. applaud.
426   *restore amends :* make
       improvements.

Classwork and Examinations

The works of Shakespeare are studied all over the world, and this classroom edition is being used in many different countries. Teaching methods vary from school to school and there are many different ways of examining a student's work. Some teachers and examiners expect detailed knowledge of Shakespeare's text; others ask for imaginative involvement with his characters and their situations; and there are some teachers who want their students to share in the theatrical experience of directing and performing a play. Most people use a variety of methods. This section of the book offers a few suggestions for approaches to *A Midsummer Night's Dream* which could be used in schools and colleges to help with students' understanding and *enjoyment* of the play.

A Discussion
B Character Study
C Activities
D Context Questions
E Comprehension Questions
F Essays
G Projects

A Discussion

Talking about the play — about the issues it raises and the characters who are involved — is one of the most rewarding and pleasurable aspects of the study of Shakespeare. It makes sense to discuss each scene as it is read, sharing impressions — and perhaps correcting misapprehensions. It can be useful to compare aspects of this play with other fictions — plays, novels, films — or with modern life.

Suggestions

A1 Egeus has chosen one man (Demetrius) for his daughter to marry, but she is in love with another (Lysander). Do you think that parents should have any influence over their daughters or sons in the choice of marriage-partners?

A2 'The course of true love never did run smooth' (*1*, 1, 134). Suggest some examples of love which has triumphed over adversity.

A3 In their 'duet' in *Act 1*, Scene 1, Lysander and Hermia enumerate various obstacles which can be encountered by lovers — perhaps they are 'different in blood', 'misgraffed in years', dependent on 'the choice of friends'. How serious do you consider any of these obstacles? Can you suggest any others?

A4 'Love looks not with the eyes, but with the mind' (*1*, 1, 234); do you think this is true?

A5 Do you believe in fairies? Compare the supernatural beings of *A Midsummer Night's Dream* with those of modern (children's) fiction, or with the creatures of science-fiction.

B   Character Study

Shakespeare is famous for his creation of characters who seem like real people. We can judge their actions and we can try to understand their thoughts and feelings — just as we criticize and try to understand the people we know. As the play progresses, we learn to like or dislike, love or hate, them — just as though they lived in *our* world.

Characters can be studied *from the outside*, by observing what they do, and listening sensitively to what they say. This is the scholar's method: the scholar — or any reader — has access to the whole play, and can see the function of every character within the whole scheme of that play.

Another approach works *from the inside*, taking a single character and looking at the action and the other characters from his/her point of view. This is an actor's technique, creating a character — who can have only a partial view of what is going on — for performance; and it asks for a student's inventive imagination. The two methods — both useful in different ways — are really complementary to each other.

Suggestions

a) from 'outside' the character

B1 Compare the characters of Demetrius and Lysander.

B2 If you were to produce the play, how would you dress Peter Quince and his fellow actors so that their costumes would indicate something about their personalities?

B3   How would you present the fairies to a modern audience?

B4   Contrast the characters of Hermia and Helena.

B5   Do you think that Helena and Demetrius deserve each other?

> b) from 'inside' a character

B6   Hippolyta is a 'foreigner' in Athens. How would she describe (in her diary, or in a letter home) the scene she has just witnessed between Egeus and his daughter?

B7   In the character of Egeus, but using your own words, ask Duke Theseus to stop the marriage of Hermia and Lysander.

B8   You are Demetrius, and you have been very quiet during the interview with Duke Theseus. Now give your account of the matter, not ignoring the accusation that you have 'made love to Nedar's daughter, Helena' (*1*, 1, 107).

B9   Write a letter from Lysander to his 'widow aunt' (*1*, 1, 156), telling her all about Hermia and about your elopement plans.

B10   As Peter Quince, write to a friend who is very interested in amateur dramatics; describe the cast you have chosen for 'Pyramus and Thisbe', and assess their chances of giving a good performance.

B11   Write another speech for the Fairy in *Act 2*, Scene 1, describing his/her activities in an urban setting.

B12   As the director of 'Pyramus and Thisbe', Peter Quince should keep a careful log-book. Write his record of the first rehearsal.

B13   In the character of Oberon, tell Titania about Puck's mistake with the love-juice.

B14   How will Puck boast to the other fairies about the way he has misled the lovers?

B15   You were present — either as a guest, a servant, or an official reporter — at the 'Athenian Wedding of the Year'. Describe everything that you saw and heard.

C   Activities

These can involve two or more students, preferably working *away from* the desk or study-table and using gesture and position ('body-language') as well as speech. They can help students to develop a sense of drama and the dramatic aspects of Shakespeare's play — which was written to be *performed*, not studied in a classroom.

Suggestions

C1 Act the play — or at least some parts of it (e.g. the performance of 'Pyramus and Thisbe').

C2 Devise an additional scene in which Theseus and Hippolyta talk about Egeus and his daughter.

C3 Improvise a scene where Egeus, talking with friends in his club, tells them about his wilful daughter, his chosen son-in-law, and his appeal to Duke Theseus.

C4 'I will go tell him of fair Hermia's flight' (*1*, 1, 246). Construct an episode in which Helena tells Demetrius of the intended elopement.

C5 Oberon wants the Indian child to be 'Knight of his train, to trace the forests wild'; but Titania 'withholds the loved boy, Crowns him with flowers, and makes him all her joy' (*2*, 1, 25–7). Give a court hearing to their appeals for custody, and adjudicate between them.

C6 The fairies — Peaseblossom, Cobweb, Moth, and Mustardseed — discuss their mistress and the monster she has fallen in love with. Improvise such a scene.

C7 As they walk back to Athens, the lovers try to recall their midsummer night's dreams (*4*, 1, 199). Enact this journey.

D Context Questions

In written examinations, these questions present you with short passages from the play, and ask you to explain them. They are intended to test your knowledge of the play and your understanding of its words. Usually you have to make a choice of passages: there may be five on the paper, and you are asked to choose three. Be very sure that you know exactly how many passages you must choose. Study the ones offered to you, and select those you feel most certain of. Make your answers accurate and concise — don't waste time writing more than the examiner is asking for.

D1 What hempen homespuns have we swaggering here,
So near the cradle of the fairy queen?

What, a play toward? I'll be an auditor —
An actor too, perhaps, if I see cause.

   (i) Who is speaking? What has he seen?
  (ii) What is the meaning of 'hempen homespuns'? Give the
      names of two of these characters.
 (iii) How does the speaker take part in the episode?

D2 I know you two are rival enemies;
How comes this gentle concord in the world,
That hatred is so far from jealousy,
To sleep by hate, and fear no enmity?

   (i) Who is the speaker, and who are the 'rival enemies'?
  (ii) What answer is the speaker given?
 (iii) How would the audience have answered the question?

D3 But, gentle friend, for love and courtesy,
Lie further off, in human modesty:
Such separation as may well be said
Becomes a virtuous bachelor and a maid,
So far be distant; and, good night, sweet friend,
Thy love ne'er alter till thy sweet life end!

   (i) Who are the 'bachelor' and the 'maid'?
  (ii) Where are they going to sleep, and why are they in this
      place?
 (iii) How and why does the love alter?

D4 Did not you tell me I should know the man
By the Athenian garments he had on?
And so far blameless proves my enterprise,
That I have 'nointed an Athenian's eyes;
And so far am I glad it so did sort,
As this their jangling I esteem a sport.

   (i) Who is speaking, and to whom? Who are the men in
      Athenian garments?
  (ii) Whose eyes have been anointed? What with?
 (iii) What is it that the speaker refers to as 'jangling'?

D5 And thorough this distemperature, we see
The seasons alter: hoary-headed frosts
Fall in the fresh lap of the crimson rose,

And on old Hiems' thin and icy crown
An odorous chaplet of sweet summer buds
Is, as in mockery, set.

(i) Who is speaking, and to whom?
(ii) What is 'old Hiems'? What has caused this situation?
(iii) What does the character addressed go on to say, and how are the words received by the speaker of the lines?

D6 I grant you, friends, if you should fright the ladies out of their wits, they would have no more discretion but to hang us; but I will aggravate my voice so that I will roar you as gently as any sucking dove; I will roar you an 'twere any nightingale.

(i) Who is the speaker? What does he want to do?
(ii) What is the speaker told he must do? How is he urged to do it?
(iii) How does the speaker respond? What question does he go on to ask?

E   Comprehension Questions

These also present passages from the play and ask questions about them, and again you often have a choice of passages. But the extracts are much longer than those presented as context questions. A detailed knowledge of the language of the play is asked for here, and you must be able to express unusual or archaic phrases in your own words; you may also be asked to comment critically on the effectiveness of Shakespeare's language.

E1 *Helena*
Have you conspir'd, have you with these contriv'd
To bait me with this foul derision?
Is all the counsel that we two have shar'd —
The sisters' vows, the hours that we have spent,
When we have chid the hasty-footed time   5
For parting us — O, is all forgot?
All school-days' friendship, childhood innocence?
We, Hermia, like two artificial gods,
Have with our needles created both one flower,
Both on one sampler, sitting on one cushion,   10
Both warbling of one song, both in one key,
As if our hands, our sides, voices, and minds,

Had been incorporate. So we grew together,
Like to a double cherry, seeming parted,
But yet a union in partition   15
Two lovely berries moulded on one stem;
So, with two seeming bodies, but one heart.

  (i) Give the exact context of this passage.
 (ii) Explain the meaning of 'incorporate' (line 13) and 'union
      in partition' (line 15).
(iii) What is meant here by the word 'artificial' (line 8)?
(iv) What does this speech show of Helena's character?

E2   *Oberon*
That very time I saw — but thou could'st not —
Flying between the cold moon and the earth,
Cupid all arm'd: a certain aim he took
At a fair vestal throned by the west
And loos'd his love-shaft smartly from his bow,   5
As it should pierce a hundred thousand hearts;
But I might see young Cupid's fiery shaft
Quench'd in the chaste beams of the wat'ry moon,
And the imperial votress pass'd on,
In maiden meditation, fancy-free.   10
Yet mark'd I where the bolt of Cupid fell:
It fell upon a little western flower,
Before milk-white, now purple with love's wound.

  (i) How important is the 'little western flower' in *A
      Midsummer Night's Dream?*
 (ii) Who is referred to in line 4?
(iii) Explain what is meant by the references to 'Cupid'.
(iv) Comment on the use of hot and cold imagery in this
      passage.

E3   *Titania*
What, wilt thou hear some music, my sweet love?
Bottom
I have a reasonable good ear in music: let's have the tongs
and the bones.
Titania
Or say, sweet love, what thou desir'st to eat.
Bottom
Truly, a peck of provender: I could munch your   5

good dry oats. Methinks I have a great desire to a bottle
of hay: good hay, sweet hay, hath no fellow.
Titania
I have a venturous fairy that shall seek
The squirrel's hoard, and fetch thee new nuts.
Bottom
I had rather have a handful or two of dried peas.   10
But, I pray you, let none of your people stir me: I have an
exposition of sleep come upon me.

  (i)   What does Bottom mean by 'the tongs and the bones'
        (lines 2–3), and 'a bottle of hay' (line 6)?
  (ii) Comment on the use of verse and prose in this passage.
  (iii) Why does Bottom say 'exposition of sleep' (line 12)? Is
        this typical of his language elsewhere in the play?

F   Essays

These will usually give you a specific topic to discuss, or perhaps a
question that must be answered, in writing, *with a reasoned argument*. They *never* want you to tell the story of the play — so don't!
Your examiner — or teacher — has read the play and does not need
to be reminded of it. Relevant quotations will always help you to
make your points more strongly.

F1   Do you think that Bottom has too much imagination — or not
enough?

F2   Give an account of the quarrel between Oberon and Titania,
identifying its causes and effects, and suggesting where *your*
sympathies lie.

F3   Compare Theseus and Hippolyta in their attitudes to the
'mechanicals' and their play.

F4   In the play, Duke Theseus is the ruler of Athens. What do we
learn about him in this capacity?

F5   'Sometimes the fairies seem very human — and at other times
they are totally alien'. Discuss.

F6   Comment on the different kinds of verse that Shakespeare
uses in this play, and the different effects he achieves.

G Projects

In some schools, students are asked to do more 'free-ranging' work, which takes them outside the text — but which should always be relevant to the play. Such Projects may demand skills other than reading and writing; design and artwork, for instance, may be involved. Sometimes a 'portfolio' of work is assembled over a considerable period of time; and this can be presented to the examiner as part of the student's work for assessment.

The availability of resources will, obviously, do much to determine the nature of the Projects; but this is something that only the local teachers will understand. However, there is always help to be found in libraries, museums, and art galleries.

G1   Puck.

G2   Fairies.

G3   The Heroes of Classical mythology.

G4   Costumes and Properties for 'Pyramus and Thisbe'.

G5   Classical allusions in *A Midsummer Night's Dream*.

Background

England c. 1595

When Shakespeare was writing *A Midsummer Night's Dream*, most people believed that the sun went round the earth. They were taught that this was a divinely ordered scheme of things, and that — in England — God had instituted a Church and ordained a Monarchy for the right government of the land and the populace.

'The past is a foreign country; they do things differently there.'

L.P. Hartley

Government

For most of Shakespeare's life, the reigning monarch of England was Queen Elizabeth I. With her counsellors and ministers she governed the country (population about five million) from London, although fewer than half a million people inhabited the capital city. In the rest of the country, law and order were maintained by the land-owners and enforced by their deputies. The average man had no vote — and his wife had no rights at all.

Religion

At this time, England was a Christian country. All children were baptized, soon after they were born, into the Church of England; they were taught the essentials of the Christian faith, and instructed in their duty to God and to humankind. Marriages were performed, and funerals conducted, only by the licensed clergy and in accordance with the Church's rites and ceremonies. Attendance at divine service was compulsory; absences (without good — medical — reason) could be punished by fines. By such means, the authorities were able to keep some check on the populace — recording births, marriages, and deaths; being alert to any religious nonconformity, which could be politically dangerous; and ensuring a minimum of orthodox instruction through the official 'Homilies' which were regularly preached from the pulpits of all parish churches throughout the realm. Following Henry VIII's break away from the Church of Rome, all people in England were able to hear the church services *in their own language*. The Book of Common Prayer was used in every church, and an English translation of the Bible was read aloud in public. The Christian religion had never been so well taught before!

Education

School education reinforced the Church's teaching. From the age of four, boys might attend the 'petty school' (French *'petite école'*) to learn the rudiments of reading and writing along with a few prayers; some schools also included work with numbers. At the age of seven, the boy was ready for the grammar school (if his father was willing and able to pay the fees). Here, a thorough grounding in Latin grammar was followed by translation work and the study of Roman authors, paying attention as much to style as to matter. The arts of fine writing were thus inculcated from early youth.

A very few students proceeded to university; these were either clever scholarship boys, or else the sons of noblemen. Girls stayed at home, and acquired domestic and social skills — cooking, sewing, perhaps even music. The lucky ones might learn to read and write.

Language

At the start of the sixteenth century the English had a very poor opinion of their own language: there was little serious writing in English, and hardly any literature. Latin was the language of international scholarship, and Englishmen admired the eloquence of the Romans. They made many translations, and in this way they extended the resources of their own language, increasing its vocabulary and stretching its grammatical structures. French, Italian, and Spanish works were also translated, and — for the first time — there were English versions of the Bible. By the end of the century, English was a language to be proud of: it was rich in synonyms, capable of infinite variety and subtlety, and ready for all kinds of word-play — especially the *puns*, for which Shakespeare's English is renowned.

Drama

The great art-form of the Elizabethan age was its drama. The Elizabethans inherited a tradition of play-acting from the Middle Ages, and they reinforced this by reading and translating the Roman playwrights. At the beginning of the sixteenth century, plays were performed by groups of actors, all-male companies (boys acted the female roles) who travelled from town to town, setting up their stages in open places (such as inn-yards) or, with the permission of the owner, in the hall of some noble house. The touring companies continued, in the provinces, into the seventeenth century; but in London, in 1576, a new building was erected for the performance of plays. This was the Theatre, the first purpose-built playhouse in England. Other playhouses followed (including Shakespeare's own theatre, the Globe); and the English drama reached new heights of eloquence.

There were those who disapproved, of course. The theatres, which brought large crowds together, could encourage the spread of disease — and dangerous ideas. During the summer, when the plague was at its worst, the playhouses were closed. A constant censorship was imposed, more or less severe at different times. The Puritan faction tried to close down the theatres, but — partly because there was royal favour for the drama, and partly because the buildings were outside the city limits — they did not succeed until 1642.

Theatre

From contemporary comments and sketches — most particularly a drawing by a Dutch visitor, Johannes de Witt — it is possible to form some idea of the typical Elizabethan playhouse for which most of Shakespeare's plays were written. Hexagonal in shape, it had three roofed galleries encircling an open courtyard. The plain, high stage projected into the yard, where it was surrounded by the audience of standing 'groundlings'. At the back were two doors for the actors' entrances and exits; and above these doors was a balcony — useful for a musicians' gallery or for the acting of scenes 'above'. Over the stage was a thatched roof, supported on two pillars, forming a canopy — which seems to have been painted with the sun, moon and stars for the 'heavens'.

Underneath was space (concealed by curtaining) which could be used by characters ascending and descending through a trap-door in the stage. Costumes and properties were kept backstage, in the 'tiring house'. The actors dressed lavishly, often wearing the secondhand clothes bestowed by rich patrons. Stage properties were important for defining a location, but the dramatist's own words were needed to explain the time of day, since all performances took place in the early afternoon.

Selected Further Reading

Interesting chapters, or essays, can be found in these books:

The Play

Barber, C.L., *Shakespeare's Festive Comedy*, (Princeton, NJ, 1959).
Briggs, K.M., *The Anatomy of Puck*, (London, 1959).
Charlton, H.B., *Shakespearian Comedy*, (London, 1939).
Dent, R.W., 'Imagination in *A Midsummer Night's Dream*', *Shakespeare Quarterly*, 15 (1964), 115–29.
Latham, M.W., *The Elizabethan Fairies*, (New York, 1930).
Leggatt, Alexander, *Shakespeare's Comedy of Love*, (London, 1974).
Salinger, Leo, *Shakespeare and the Traditions of Comedy*, (Cambridge, 1974).

Background Reading

Blake, N.F., *Shakespeare's Language: an Introduction*, (Methuen, 1983).
Muir, K., and Schoenbaum, S., *A New Companion to Shakespeare Studies*, (Cambridge, 1971).
Schoenbaum, S., *William Shakespeare: A Documentary Life*, (Oxford, 1975).
Thomson, Peter, *Shakespeare's Theatre*, (Routledge and Kegan Paul, 1983).

William Shakespeare, 1564-1616

Elizabeth I was Queen of England when Shakespeare was born in 1564. He was the son of a tradesman who made and sold gloves in the small town of Stratford-upon-Avon, and he was educated at the grammar school in that town. Shakespeare did not go to university when he left school, but worked, perhaps, in his father's business. When he was eighteen he married Anne Hathaway, who became the mother of his daughter, Susanna, in 1583, and of twins in 1585.

There is nothing exciting, or even unusual, in this story; and from 1585 until 1592 there are no documents that can tell us anything at all about Shakespeare. But we have learned that in 1592 he was known in London, and that he had become both an actor and a playwright.

We do not know when Shakespeare wrote his first play, and indeed we are not sure of the order in which he wrote his works. If you look on page 97 at the list of his writings and their approximate dates, you will see how he started by writing plays on subjects taken from the history of England. No doubt this was partly because he was always an intensely patriotic man—but he was also a very shrewd business-man. He could see that the theatre audiences enjoyed being shown their own history, and it was certain that he would make a profit from this kind of drama.

The plays in the next group are mainly comedies, with romantic love stories of young people who fall in love with one another and, at the end of the play, marry and live happily ever after.

At the end of the sixteenth century the happiness disappears, and Shakespeare's plays become melancholy, bitter, and tragic. This change may have been caused by some sadness in the writer's life (one of his twins died in 1596). Shakespeare, however, was not the only writer whose works at this time were very serious. The whole of England was facing a crisis. Queen Elizabeth I was growing old. She was greatly loved, and the people were sad to think she must soon die; they were also afraid, for the Queen had never married, and so there was no child to succeed her.

When James I came to the throne in 1603, Shakespeare continued to write serious drama—the great tragedies and the plays based on Roman history (such as *Julius Caesar*) for which he is most famous. Finally, before he retired from the theatre, he wrote another set of comedies. These all have the same theme: they tell of happiness which is lost, and then found again.

Shakespeare returned from London to Stratford, his home town. He was rich and successful, and he owned one of the biggest houses in the town. He died in 1616.

Shakespeare also wrote two long poems, and a collection of sonnets. The sonnets describe two love-affairs, but we do not know who the lovers were. Although there are many public documents concerned with his career as a writer and a business-man, Shakespeare has hidden his personal life from us. A nineteenth-century poet, Matthew Arnold, addressed Shakespeare in a poem, and wrote 'We ask and ask—Thou smilest, and art still'.

There is not even a trustworthy portrait of the world's greatest dramatist.